T0209229

MY Forever Memories OF YOU

Place photo of your loved one here

MY *Forever* Memories OF YOU

The Story of our Relationship

Discovering Eternal Hope in the Midst of Grief

Written by

Eva Juliuson

And you

WESTBOW
P R E S S®
A DIVISION OF THOMAS NELSON
& ZONDERVAN

THE HOLY BIBLE, NEW INTERNATIONAL VERSION®, NIV® Copyright © 1973, 1978, 1984, 2011 by Biblica, Inc.® Used by permission. All rights reserved worldwide.

WestBow Press books may be ordered through booksellers or by contacting:

WestBow Press
A Division of Thomas Nelson & Zondervan
1663 Liberty Drive
Bloomington, IN 47403
www.westbowpress.com
1 (866) 928-1240

Print information available on the last page.

ISBN: 978-1-9736-0677-2 (sc)
ISBN: 978-1-9736-0676-5 (e)

Library of Congress Control Number: 2017917446

WestBow Press rev. date: 11/15/2017

This book is dedicated:

To Jesus Christ, who willingly sacrificed His life so death is not the end;

To Steven Hall, my late husband who suffered so others could grow deeper in the Lord;

To Dwight Juliuson, my present husband who selflessly encouraged me to publish this book;

And to you.

I pray this book will help you labor through your grief and find new life ahead.

Introduction

my letter to you

Dear Friend,

I'm so sorry for your pain. Whether you just lost a child, your spouse, a parent, a sibling, or a dear friend; you probably feel as though your whole world has collapsed. You fear you will never be the same. You're right. You won't be. As you work through the most difficult challenge you may ever face, may you grow in peace and hope as you recover from your heartbreak. It can be a very difficult and lonely climb up out of the deep abyss of grief. You may wonder if you can ever survive the pain. The death of a loved one cuts deep into your soul. I know. My husband died at the age of 37, leaving me behind with four children to raise by myself.

Around the time of Steve's death, there was a story on national television which I identified with. There were Siamese twin baby girls whose bodies were joined together from the chest to a leg. When one turned to reach for a toy, the other followed in perfect synchronization. They were separate individuals, yet they were one. Watching the videos of their first two years of life, I noticed the love in their eyes as they glanced at one another, sharing a language and bond no one else could understand. Their parents couldn't begin to imagine them apart.

When they were two years old, their doctors decided they were ready to be surgically separated. The operation saved one twin's life, but the other sister died. The parents and doctors told the interviewer how worried they were for the surviving twin. The once-lively little girl moped around looking for her other half, not knowing how to live without her. The little girl wouldn't eat or talk. No one knew how her deep grief would affect her recovery from such an intensive separation.

I felt her pain. It was my own. Steve and I had spent 22 years of life together. We started dating at 15 years old and never had any other serious boyfriend or girlfriend. After high school, we couldn't wait to get married and start our life together. That life included four children, working side-by-side in a business, and facing a terminal illness together.

We enjoyed being a team. We could read each other's thoughts and met every trial and joy together. When Steve became increasingly ill, we faced insurmountable physical, emotional and financial challenges. We dealt with them truly connected in our very souls.

When he died, it seemed I had been cut apart with no anesthesia for the pain. A huge bleeding wound remained where my husband once stood by my side. I looked for him, grieving his absence, not knowing how I could ever go on in this life without him. I knew I would never be the same. I'm not.

The Lord healed those deep wounds I thought would never quit bleeding, and then led me to counsel others in grief for over 20 years now. Your wounds will also heal. There will always be a deep scar to remind you of the eternal love for your loved one. You will also comfort others with a depth of compassion the unscarred cannot. That scar serves as a permanent reminder to cherish each moment and person in our life.

This book is written with love so you may know you *will* survive your grief. You will live again. There will even come a time when you will be happy again. The joy will be even greater, because of the sorrow you are experiencing now.

It's true—your life will never be the same, but there's no need to fear. You are being led into new territories by the One who knows the way. You may have lost the person that you depended on most in life. Now is the time to depend on God! He knows we are torn apart by death; but He views death as the sweet homecoming of one of His precious children to an eternal life filled with joy and love that we can't even imagine.

There is no way to get away from the pain; but grieving with hope means trusting the Lord to get you through the gut-wrenching trauma of being torn apart from the one you love. Don't be afraid. As you work through all your overwhelming emotions with God's help, may you discover an ever-deepening relationship with Him that will more than fill the huge vacuum left in your heart.

If I could, I would give you a big hug right now, for hugs are often more comforting than words. Since I can't be there, please accept these words of hope and encouragement as my hug and prayer for you. May you experience Jesus' loving arms around you, comforting you and holding you up when you feel you can't go on. Hold on to Him for dear life as you go through your grief.

What happened to the little surviving Siamese twin? It was kind of strange. I finally got to the point in my life where I was healing from my grief. Several years later, I saw a follow-up report on her. (I happened to be sitting next to the man who I would re-marry…but that's a whole new story.) The little girl had undergone more surgeries, extensive treatments and therapy to reconstruct her body. She had been fitted with a prosthetic leg since she had shared legs with her twin. She was giddily sprinting around looking for adventure, her face glowing with excitement. She had undergone some intense healing of her own! I'm sure she will always think of her twin as she goes on with her life. The scars will always be there to prove they were once joined together physically—and will be forever joined in spirit.

Someday there will be a tremendous reunion when those twins embrace once again in Heaven. Someday, we will all be reunited with our Lord and our loved ones. It will be *glorious*! In the meantime, we still have more life to live here, until it's our time to go. Our journey begins with God helping us through the intense grief in front of us. This book has been bathed in prayer for you. Use it. Write in it. Pray in it. The life in front of you can seem hopeless and dark without your loved one. Take this book with you as you travel through this dark valley. I will try to help you along the way. However, God is the One who can help you do the impossible—go through your grief and have an even deeper richer life in front of you.

If God can heal that little girl (and me) from our wounds, He will surely be there to help you recover, as well. Go ahead and grieve—but grieve with hope.

With love and prayer,
Eva

"Praise be to the God and Father of our Lord Jesus Christ, the Father of compassion and the God of all comfort, who comforts us in all our troubles, so that we can comfort those in any trouble with the comfort we ourselves have received from God."

2 Corinthians 1:3-4

Comfort At Last
Written by Steven D.Hall (my first husband)

Into His arms I fall
And I shall suffer nevermore.
He has truly heard my call
And led me to his door.

From the pain He's set me free.
I find comfort in his home.
He has truly heard my need
From His flock I shall not roam.

From a life unkind He saves my soul
And I walk now at His side.
I have become the wind that blows
For on his wings I ride.

As I breathe my final breath,
True peace is what I find.
With Him now, I shall rest.
Only my body I leave behind.

When a tear falls from your eyes
And you're feeling all alone,
The comfort you feel shall be I.
For you, I wait within his home.

What Happened?

"With a loud cry, Jesus breathed His last. The curtain of the temple was torn in two from top to bottom" Mark 15:37-38 (Just like our lives are torn in two when our loved one die—but it's not the end!)

Sharing Our Experiences

MUCH OF THIS book will be written by you, telling your story of your relationship. This book begins at the point of their death, because that's what you are dealing with now. The shock and finality of death can be extremely challenging to deal with. You may find yourself reliving and retelling the traumatic story of their passing from this life to the next. It might have been expected due to a prolonged illness. It could have totally taken you by surprise as in a sudden accident. It could have been deeply violent such as a suicide or murder. Part of dealing with your grief is to face their moment of death. There are times the trauma keeps replaying as you deal with flashbacks which take you back to that moment (especially if it didn't seem to be peaceful.)

This first chapter focuses on those moments. However, that particular moment is only a fraction of your entire relationship with your loved one. As you move through this section, I urge you to not get stuck here forever. Keep going for you want to have a full picture of your relationship with the dear one you are grieving. Your relationship consists of much more than that moment of death—no matter what the cause was.

I share parts of my story and others' grief throughout this book to give you an idea of how to write openly and honestly about your loved one. The most critical part of this book is *your* story of what your loved one means to you—and reaching out to God who truly knows and loves you. Feel free to take as much time as you want on each chapter, or skip around depending on what you are going through at the time. Don't try to speed through this book, but go slowly through each part at your own pace. This book is designed not just to be read, but to work through. That involves much more than simple reading. It means honestly sharing your heart.

Take whatever information seems to help you and skip over what doesn't seem to pertain. These are real tools to help you through your grief. It really does help to work through your memories and not avoid them. If you are grieving the loss of a baby or child, you may not have as many memories to hang on to, so you may fill out the memories you were looking forward to sharing with them.

I have often wished I could take away grievers' pain, but I know I cannot. It is proof of the love they shared with that person. Through the years, I have watched people I care about work through the intense pain of grief until it gives way to joyful abundant life which includes all the best their loved one left them with. It will take some time, work and pain, but I pray this happens for you as you work through your time of grief.

My Story- What Happened:

It seemed like an ordinary morning-at least as ordinary as it got in our household of four children, along with six extra children in my licensed childcare home and my husband's devastating illness. Steve had seemed better the last month, though. He had been able to truly enjoy Christmas for the first time in years. Even New Year's Eve had been a non-traumatic celebration. It had only been one year ago- last New Year's Eve, he had "died" in my arms. The Code team had revived him last year and he had endured a month of hell on life support. My courageous husband fought back from that episode to be able to walk again. Steve was an expert at battling by that time; he had been in the hospital 40 times in the prior three years and a lot of those were spent in Intensive Care Units. We were elated that he had made it through another year. The last month had actually been a surprisingly good one.

After the last near-death experience, we finally had everything he needed set up at home with home health care. We wanted to spend every possible moment together in our own home. He was sick of hospitals. We all were. Steve wanted to be around his own family, complete with the smells of home-cooking and the sounds of noisy children playing. The kids got to see their dad more often in a more natural setting- our crazy house. I could continue my work, taking care of children in my licensed child care home. I could also care for Steve and our children and attempt some kind of normalcy.

The night before was a very special evening. Looking back, he was preparing us. Without a word, Steve gathered energy to do what he had been unable to do for years. He fixed dinner for me and our two youngest boys. Our two-year old and seven year-old sons rode his back like a horse. The past year kept us all on constant vigil with his constant falls; now here he was rough-housing with his sons like the healthy Steve we used to know.

I sat exhausted but happy in the recliner, watching the scene. He went and got a blanket and tenderly covered me up. That night we stayed up long after the kids were asleep expressing our feelings for each other and his concerns for my future. He commented he was really tired of fighting and didn't think he could keep going much longer. We had faced death so many times, so that conversation seemed nothing new to me (We had talked often about his death)…or perhaps the reality of his impending death was more than I could acknowledge.

The next morning, I began the morning ritual of welcoming the child care kids as they arrived for the day. The house was full of our kids mixed with other children who had just finished breakfast. I was getting the older kids ready for school. I had just checked on Steve ten minutes earlier and he was sleeping peacefully. When I opened the bedroom door to let him know I was loading the kids up to take to school, that's when I knew. He was gone.

He looked beautiful—fully dressed in jeans, boots, and a brand new sweater he had gotten for Christmas. He always dressed in clothes during the day instead of pajamas, no matter how bad he felt. It was his way of not letting the disease beat him down. I shouldn't be surprised that he dressed to leave this world. He looked so peaceful—but he was gone! *He was gone.* This time he was gone for sure. The world stood still. What would I do?

"Blessed are those who mourn. They will be comforted." Matthew 5:4

Your Story- What Happened?

Write your story here. Tell what happened the day your loved one died. Don't worry about spelling or punctuation. Just write honestly from your heart.

_____

_____

_____

_____

_____

_____

_____

_____

_____

_____

_____

_____

_____

_____

_____

_____

_____

_____

_____

_____

_____

"Jesus answered him, 'I tell you the truth, today you will be with Me in paradise.'" Luke 23:43

Helpful Input- What Happened?

"Blessed are those who mourn. They will be comforted." Matthew 5:4

You may not be able to tell everyone what happened to your loved one right away…but it is important to tell your story. Yes, it will be painful. Telling what happened helps you work through it and absorb the reality that your loved one is no longer physically with you. The pain needs to come out. Telling your story is part of your healing.

Many people are afraid if they ever start telling, they will never be able to stop crying. I've often heard grievers say they are afraid they will completely lose it. During the course of grieving, most people discover the anxiety of facing something can be worse than actually doing it. The full story of the relationship between the griever and their loved one most often comes out in bits and pieces. It can seem too much to bear all at once. I believe that the numbness we feel at first is part of God's protection during our healing process. We can only handle so much pain in our fresh raw state.

Find a safe person to tell the first time you share your story– someone who will truly listen all the way through without interruptions or advice. Sometimes it's easier to write it down first. You can voice the whole story with no one else's comments or questions inserted. It just needs to come out! The design of this book breaks up your story into sections so you can deal with various parts of your story when you are ready.

Sometimes people think if they don't talk about it, it won't hurt or they won't have to deal with it. There is no way around it. Sooner or later, you have to go through it. As painful as it is, you will survive the worst part of your grief and come out much healthier if you face it and ask God to help you work through it. It's like holding your broken-in-a-million-pieces heart up to Him and asking Him to heal it.

Not everyone wants to hear your story. Many people don't know how to respond, or they can't handle your pain. Find someone who is a really good listener. More than anything, you need someone who will let you vocalize what you are going through without telling you that you shouldn't feel a certain way.

One of the best things about writing your story is that you can get it all out without interruption or analysis. Even though it may seem that you are alone in your writing and pain, God is with you. He's the best listener of all. He's never too busy. He is not distracted. Nothing is too hard for Him to handle. He is there when no one else is—day and night. He will always understand you better than anyone else.

"The Lord is close to the broken-hearted and saves those who are crushed in spirit." Psalm 34:18

As time goes on, you may feel like you're repeating the same story over and over. You may worry some of your friends will tire of hearing it. You are doing what you need to do to process what has happened. Keep telling it. Sometimes you may find yourselves telling a clerk at the store or a stranger on the phone. Tell your story to whomever you need to. Not only is it helping you; you never know how God is using it to help someone else!

Don't worry about feeling the correct emotions when you tell what happened. You may feel nothing; other times, it will cut incredibly deep. Sometimes it seems like a bad dream; like you're talking about something horrible that happened to someone else. Sometimes you find yourself laughing nervously—though it's horrific!

Family and friends are also grieving. Sharing with them can help you work through your grief together. Even children need to process what has happened. Let them see you cry so they know it's OK to feel the emotions. You are not protecting them by hiding your pain. Do reassure them that you will be alright; that you are sad from missing your loved one; that you just need to cry. See more about children in chapter "Helping Children Grieve." Tell them you need a hug. They need one, too!

> *"Brothers, we do not want you to be ignorant about those who fall asleep, or to grieve like the rest of men, who have no hope." 1 Thessalonians 4:13*

Practical Ideas- What Happened?

> *"I am convinced that nothing can ever separate us from God's love which Jesus Christ our Lord shows us. We can't be separated by death or life, by angels or rulers, by anything in the present or anything in the future, by forces or powers in the world above or in the world below, or by anything else in creation." Romans 8:38–39*

- Write in this book. Put your favorite photo of your loved one on the front. This will be a book of your personal journey through grief.
- Start a blog and share your grief with others. It may help them as much as you.
- Find a good grief support group where you can share

Compassionate Friends for parents who've lost a child
Grief Share is a biblical-based group that offers free helpful daily emails for a year
Grief Recovery has groups and individual counselors
Local churches, hospitals and funeral homes sometimes have groups available

- Share your story with a group who already knows you (a small group or Sunday School class at church, a team, or a group of friends or co-workers)

- Sometimes you can meet with someone you know who is also going through a recent loss. We have a group of widows who meet weekly at our church.

- If your story involves a tragedy that might help someone else- think about sharing it to prevent other deaths or help survivors of suicide, substance abuse, safety issues, infant or other deaths. Of course, not everyone can share their grief in such a public manner.

- Gather family and friends so everyone can tell what they were going through when your loved one died.

- Help children involved tell their story through drawings, playing out with stuffed animals, or writing. Don't force them; just give them the opportunity. See chapter on Children. Better yet, get a copy of the companion book My Forever Memories for children.

- If someone keeps interrupting or telling you how you should or shouldn't feel, try not to get too upset. That person means well; they probably just don't understand. You may need to find someone else to share with who will listen without judgement.

- Try not to avoid the pain through excessive use of meds, alcohol, entertainment, work, busy-ness, other relationships, drugs, or food. It is good to take little breaks from intense grief, but there's no way to completely avoid the pain. The best way to get through it is to go through it.

- Your story is yours. No one has ever had a relationship like yours before. It's one-of-a-kind. Therefore, no one else can truly comprehend what you are going through except for God who sees deeply into each of our souls and who knows us better than we know ourselves.

"For I know the plans I have for you,' declares the Lord, 'plans to prosper you and not to harm you, plans to give you hope and a future. Then you will call upon Me and come and pray to Me, and I will listen to you. You will seek Me and find Me when you seek Me with all your heart.'" Jeremiah 29:11-13

Interactive Work page- What happened?

"Even though I walk through the dark valley of death, because You are with me, I fear no harm. Your rod and staff give me courage." Psalm 23:4

- What were you doing the day your loved one died?

_____

_____

- What happened in that moment of passing/ or when you first heard the news?

_____

_____

- Who was with your loved one? Who was with you?

_____

_____

- When did it happen? Was it expected or unexpected?

_____

_____

- How did you feel? How did you react? How did others react?

_____

_____

- How has your life changed?

_____

_____

"Precious in the sight of the Lord is the death of His faithful ones." Psalm 116:15

Prayer Journal- What Happened?

"He is not the God of the dead, but of the living, for to Him all are alive." Luke 20:38

My Prayer Journal (excerpts from my prayer journal):

Oh, God!

Not now! Not now! He's gone. I'm not ready! I thought I was prepared for this- I'm not! I just checked on him. How could he be gone? Are you still in the room, Steve? You aren't in your body. You have to be somewhere!

CPR!!! Should I try to revive you or let you be? You've suffered so long. You look so peaceful. Perhaps I should just let you go. I've got to try. That's why I learned CPR- for you…for a time like this! Can I live with myself if I don't?

I have to try, even though I know it won't make any difference. This time you're gone for sure. Start CPR. I hope I remember how.

Call Chrissy!!! (our 15 year-old daughter in the next room) "Chrissy, call 911!"

Oh, God! Help her. Please, help her! Chrissy's falling apart! I can't help her and Steve right now. My heart is broken. I can't remember CPR! Just do it! His lips are lifeless. He really is gone. He's not coming back.

Steve, I know you are watching me. You're gone! Oh, God! I've broken your rib with the CPR! I'm so sorry, honey! You don't care, do you? It's not important. You can no longer feel pain. You're really gone! My tears are mixing with yours. You have two tears in your eyes! You were thinking of us when you died, weren't you?

God, please take care of my love. He's not coming back. Keep compressing his chest!

Here are the paramedics! Strange- I'm totally calm. He's not coming back. They're ripping his clothes off to try to revive him. I should have made them leave him alone. He looked so beautiful. This is not real—yet it is.

At the Hospital right after his death:

Father, he looks so peaceful. He's still so warm. His color even looks good. There's so much peace in this room. This is a holy place and a holy time! He just left this earth for heaven. His pain and suffering are over. He fought the good fight and now he's finished.

Next time I see his body, it will be cold. Right now, he's still so warm. I don't want to leave him. I don't want to leave this holy time. I place my hand on his warm neck and hold his hand. Here is my love—this body I know so well and have cared for… yet he is gone.

We knew this time was coming. It's okay. Peace and warmth. I've been in lots of hospital rooms, emergency rooms and intensive care units with my love. Never before has there been this much peace and warmth. Thank you, Lord.

"He is the healer of the brokenhearted. He is the one who bandages their wounds." Psalm 147:3

Your Prayer Journal- What Happened?

Don't worry about spelling or punctuation, just write your prayer about what happened the day of your loved one's death

_____

_____

_____

_____

_____

_____

_____

_____

_____

_____

_____

_____

_____

_____

_____

_____

_____

_____

_____

_____

_____

"Don't be afraid; because I am with you. Don't be intimidated: I am your God. I will strengthen you. I will help you. I will support you with my victorious right hand."

Isaiah 41:10

2

The World Should Stop!

"It was now about the sixth hour, and darkness came over the whole land until the ninth hour, for the sun stopped shining. And the curtain of the temple was torn in two. Jesus called out in a loud voice, 'Father, into Your hands I commit my spirit.' When he had said this, he breathed his last." Luke 23:44-46

Sharing Our Experiences

MY EXPERIENCES WILL be completely different than yours because you are completely different than me, and there's never been anyone else exactly like our loved ones—not ever before, not now and or ever again! I share my experience with you so you'll know someone else has made it through grief and so that you'll know I understand and care about you. No one should try to compare whose grief is worse or more intense. It's your grief. No one else has shared the unique relationship you had with the one you love. This grief you are experiencing is not so much for your loved one because their pain and suffering are finished. We grieve for ourselves as we experience the huge void they left in our lives.

Perhaps some of my experience might put voice to something you are feeling that you didn't even realize. It's still not your own experience, though. That's why it is so important to work through your own emotions and experiences, and try to express them in the best way you can. Sharing our heart's deepest thoughts helps us to process and learn from them. Sharing our deepest, most honest prayers with the Lord God, who created us and knows us better than we know ourselves, will help us begin to heal.

I write to share with you. May you write to share with God.

My Story- The World Should Stop!

Driving back to the church from the graveside the day of the funeral, I looked out the window of the limo at people going to work and running errands. I wanted to scream, "The world should stop!"

I looked at my poor children sitting quietly in the seats next to me and thought, "Our world has stopped." Yet everyone was going about their normal day as if nothing had happened. They had no idea.

The world should stop because the love of my life had died! The world should stop so I could comprehend what just happened. The world should stop so I could help my children. The world should stop because it would never be the same again. The world should stop because I had no idea how to go on!

Policemen might have stopped traffic on the way to the cemetery, but it sped by faster than ever on the way back. How could life go on as usual? We drove back to the church for a memorial dinner where friends and family gathered. We had brought photo albums to share. That took away the harsh reality for a bit as we all reminisced about fun times with Steve. Laughter and hugs were passed around. Then slowly people began to get up and head for the door to return to their everyday lives.

Someone had taken the kids back to our house to hang out with cousins. There were only a few people remaining, and they were all busy cleaning up. I sat in utter shock. I think I probably looked ok on the outside, but I was completely lost on the inside. I had no idea where to go or what to do. I've never been so *lost*. I sat stunned, immovable. What seemed like hours of paralysis was probably only a few moments. Then I suddenly remembered my children were at home and needed me. I made myself get up and drive home. Although—I do not recall the drive.

Later that same day (The day of the funeral), I answered the phone when it rang. It was one of many bill collectors. We owed over a million dollars' worth of medical bills at the time of Steve's death. It had become part of our everyday life to deal with bill collectors. As you can imagine, we had struggled financially nonstop throughout his expensive illness. The collector started in his spiel. I interrupted him to let him know I had just buried my husband that day. He didn't seem to care one bit and continued rudely pushing for money. I hung up on him, but was once again reminded the world was not going to stop to let me grieve.

The world might not stop, but I knew I needed to take time to grieve. Although I had to keep working to provide for my family, I could go slowly and take time to review the most meaningful relationship I had ever had. Even though I had to drive kids to school, cook, clean and take care of bills, I could still take this time in my life to realize how blessed I had been to have Steve in my life. I needed to look back over the meaning of his life, and to realize the great impact he had on me and others.

The world might not stop, but I was going to take time to cherish his life as I grieved.

"I thank my God every time I remember you." Philippians 1:3

Your Story- The World Should Stop!

Write about your feelings of being left behind without your loved one. It doesn't have to make sense or be in any order. Just write!

_____

_____

_____

_____

_____

_____

_____

_____

_____

_____

_____

_____

_____

_____

_____

_____

_____

_____

_____

_____

_____

_____

_____
_____
_____
_____
_____
_____
_____
_____
_____
_____
_____
_____
_____
_____
_____
_____
_____
_____
_____
_____
_____
_____
_____
_____
_____
_____
_____
_____

"Do not be terrified; do not be discouraged, for the Lord your God will be with you wherever you go." Joshua 1:9b

Helpful Input- The World Should Stop!

"When you pass through the waters, I will be with you; and when you pass through the rivers, they will not sweep over you." Isaiah 43:2

The world definitely doesn't stop for you to grieve, but you need to allow yourself the time and give yourself permission to. Of course, your grief will take on a different look than others' because of who you are—and who you are grieving.

Grief often comes in waves—torrential tsunamis at first. It washes over you, taking your breath, causing you to feel like you will literally drown. You may look ok on the outside, but inside you are grasping to hold on to something solid. Some show it more on the outside, as well. Panic. Gasping. Real fears that you will drown in grief. Many times, you truly wonder if you will live through the crashing pounding waves that threaten to overtake you. Then it passes; at least giving you a momentary breather.

Then you hear a song, smell their clothes, catch a glimpse of a photo that brings on another crashing wave. Will you drown in your grief, in your tears? Hold on and ride the wave. After the first several bouts of waves, you realize that they will not kill you. Just as there is a beginning, there is also an end to the wave. As you travel through your grief, you will slowly begin to realize the waves begin to get smaller with a little more time in between waves. It helps so much to hold on to the Lord as those waves crash over you. Write to Him. Tell Him what you are going through. He will never leave you.

"I will turn the rivers into islands and dry up the pools. I will lead the blind by ways they have not known, along unfamiliar paths I will guide them; I will turn the darkness into light before them and make the rough places smooth. These are the things I will do; I will not forsake them." Isaiah 42:15b-16

Even when our loved ones have to leave us, God never will. He is faithful to stay with us as we travel through the rough waters of grief. He doesn't take it away, but leads us through. He walks through the valley of the shadow of death with us. We won't always have to stay there, but we must travel through. There is no way around it. The more we avoid it, the longer it will take to go through.

No one else can fully understand our grief—the pain we are experiencing—the fear of being left behind. God does. He knows us deeper than we know ourselves. He knows the help we need. Our Lord doesn't ever leave us alone in this world. He is with us no matter what we face.

Though our loved ones have passed from the troubles and trials of this world, we have not. We still have to face each day along with whatever comes our way. There are still taxes, bills, meals, health issues, children, other relationships, repairs… and much more that must be dealt with. The world doesn't wait until we are ready to handle those things. Life keeps happening. God is with us to help us through each day. It's easy to start thinking too far ahead. How you will handle all the rest of your life without your loved one? To face it all at once can be overwhelming. Yet we are made to go slowly and lightly through life, trusting that God is with us, giving us what we need for each day.

You may be missing your loved one more than you thought possible, but God will more than fill the huge void they left in your life. He helps you through your grief by helping you fully realize the precious gift He gave you in your loved one. Then He begins to help you see that He is there to fill that huge hole with Himself through the gift He gave you in Jesus Christ. Keep turning to the Lord through your grief and He will bring you out into new life. Even when the world doesn't stop, the Lord will stop with you and help you through.

"I will not leave you as orphans; I will come to you." John 14:18

Practical Ideas- The World Should Stop!

"In this world you will have trouble. But take heart! I have overcome the world." John 16:33b

- Take time to grieve by looking through photos, letters, cards. Appreciate the love you shared.
- Take a break from grieving by doing something fun.(Yet don't use constant entertainment to avoid grieving)
- Listen to music you both liked.
- Let others know you need time to grieve. If they invite you somewhere, let them know you may not be up to it when the time comes. Grief can cause a change of emotions as often as every few minutes for a while.
- List things you are thankful to have shared with your loved one.
- Thank God for the great qualities you saw in your loved one.
- Be easy on yourself as you face daily challenges without your loved one. Realize it will not always be this hard.
- Gather good advice on handling issues without your loved one. Once you have counsel, pray about it and take your time making decisions. Don't let others rush you.
- When possible, postpone any major decisions for at least a year such as selling your house, car, moving out of state. There are real life situations when this is not possible. Be sure to pray your way through.
- Listen to Christian music; read scripture; have daily devotions (GriefShare sends out great free daily devotions for grievers in the form of emails)
- Don't give your loved one's personal items away until you are ready. Make sure the timing is right for you.
- Try to realize others have to go forward in their lives and can't completely stop for yours.
- Take time to pray and write in a prayer journal every day. God has all eternity to listen and is never too busy.

"My grace is sufficient for you, for My power is made perfect in weakness." 2 Corinthians 12:9

Interactive Workpage- The World Should Stop!

"But seek first his kingdom and his righteousness, and all these things will be given to you as well. Therefore do not worry about tomorrow, for tomorrow will worry about itself. Each day has enough trouble of its own." Matthew 6:33–34

- How can I set aside time to grieve every day for a while? (work through this book, write in a prayer journal, take a quiet walk each day…)

_____

_____

- Who do I need to let know that I need to grieve *my* way?

_____

_____

- What decisions do I have to make now?

_____

_____

- What decisions can I wait on?

_____

_____

- Which areas do I need immediate help with? (paying bills, balancing checkbook, lowering bills..)

_____

_____

- Can I, or do I want to take time off from work? How long? (Realize you will not be as productive for a while. Great amounts of energy are required to grieve)

_____

_____

- What activities can I cut back on to make it easier to go through grief?

_____

_____

- Which activities do I want to maintain to keep a daily routine going?

_____

_____

"Even though I walk through the valley of the shadow of death, I will fear no evil, for You are with me; Your rod and Your staff, they comfort me." Psalm 23:4

Prayer Journal- The World Should Stop!

"In the same way, the Spirit helps us in our weakness. We do not know what we ought to pray for, but the Spirit himself intercedes for us with groans that words cannot express. And he who searches our hearts knows the mind of the Spirit, because the Spirit intercedes for the saints in accordance with God's will." Romans 8:26-27

My Prayer Journal- The World Should Stop!

(note- These prayers contain combined excerpts from my personal prayer journal. My unedited prayer journals often ramble or repeat out of urgency--so if yours do, don't worry. Pour your heart out to the Lord)

Father,

My world has been torn in two… before and after Steve's death! I am incredibly weak and fragile. Does anybody realize how frail I am? It's like being run over by a semi-truck. Maybe if I was in a wreck, people would understand my wounds. I hear a lot of people say that I look good. Sometimes that just makes me mad. *I am not OK*! Yet I know I will be. I don't even know how to answer when people ask how I'm doing. I don't even know how I'm doing. I'm trusting You, Lord, to hold my hand through this chaotic time. I am used to crying out to You. How else would I have made it through Steve's all-consuming illness the last 4 years? You are my stability, my Rock, my anchor! I am holding on to You for dear life to keep from going under.

Lord, I took the kids to a science museum. My heart was not in it but they needed a break. They had a huge exhibition of Native American artifacts. The kids ran ahead, having fun, doing their own thing. I was so glad they could have a break from grieving for a while. Yet, it is in those quiet moments that I grieve the most. My eyes were drawn to a beautiful woven shawl. As I stopped to read about it, tears flowed. It was titled "The Widow's Shawl." When a woman lost her husband, she wore this shawl for at least a year, longer if needed. Everyone in the tribe knew she needed extra care and help during this time. They were careful with her, realizing the tremendous toll of grief. How I wish I had a shawl like that. I wouldn't need to explain. Everyone would just know to be gentle. (Perhaps if I wore a sign?) But the world doesn't stop! I'm just so grateful that You understand what I cannot express, Lord!

The hugs without words are the best gift people can give me… or a card with a prayer.

Well-meaning advice brings out an ugly anger in me that I don't like. I know they mean well. I've had to tell a few people to let *me* take care of *my* kids through this. They are *my* family! Other people do not know what is best for my children. I may seem weak, but You have given me a mother's love for my kids. I know they need me! We will get through this as a family. I will not let my family fall apart after all we've been through. Yet I know I need *Your* strength, Lord. I cannot be mother and father to them. I cannot be a dad, no matter how hard I try. But You can. You promise to be the father to the fatherless. I'm counting on You to provide, protect, guide and teach my children. They are Your children even before they were Steve's (or mine!)

Oh God! How I miss Steve's companionship, his input, his hugs, his wisdom. He was always there to help me face any trial or obstacle (even in his illness). We decided together how to handle situations with our kids; in business; with finances; house and car repairs…Can't the world stop with all these decisions that must be made? Doesn't the world understand I can't handle this much in the state I am in? I'm going to rely on You where I relied on Steve before. You will need to be my husband. I am trusting You will comfort me, guide me, provide for me, understand me and coax me.

So much in the world seems petty and insignificant now. What does having material things mean in the scheme of eternity? Lord, please use this time in my life to cut out things that don't matter and to add what is eternal and lasting.

Heavenly Father, the world may not stop for me to come to terms with Steve's absence…but You are always there as I take stops with You each day. I could never face this without You.

> *"As it is, you do not belong to the world, but I have chosen you out of the world."*
> *John 15:19b*

Your Prayer Journal- The World Should Stop!

(Write in your prayer journal about how your world has stopped with the death of your loved one. Don't worry about what to say…just start writing)

_____

_____

_____

_____

_____

_____

_____

_____

_____

_____

_____

_____

_____

_____

_____

_____

_____

_____

_____

_____

_____

_____

_____
_____
_____
_____
_____
_____
_____
_____
_____
_____
_____
_____
_____
_____
_____
_____
_____
_____
_____
_____
_____
_____
_____
_____
_____

_"Those who sow in tears will reap with songs of joy. He who goes out weeping, carrying
no seed to sow, will return with songs of joy, carrying sheaves with him." Psalm
126:5-6_

Am I Going Crazy?

"I am confined and cannot escape; my eyes are dim with grief. I call to You, O Lord every day; I spread out my hands to You." Psalm 88:8b-9

Sharing Our Experiences- Am I Going Crazy?

THROUGH THE YEARS I have listened to grievers, I am almost certain every single person has questioned their sanity at some point in their journey through grief. Because so many others have voiced this concern, it somehow seems more normal. What if others had not shared their experience? It shows how important it is to try to voice what you are going through in some manner. Otherwise, you might be adding all those unnamed, unmentioned emotions, fears and worries to the already heavy load you are carrying.

Sharing all your thoughts, concerns and burdens with the Lord allows you to hold them all before Him and actually give them to Him one by one, as you name them. He never designed us to carry such heavy loads by ourselves. He is always waiting to take our load as we bring it to Him. Because every single day brings with it new things to handle, we need to openly share each day's burdens…or we might indeed go crazy over carrying much more than we were meant to bear.

My Story- Am I Going Crazy?

Without realizing what I was doing, the steering wheel turned the corner and pulled into the parking lot of the Lupus Association office. I ran in and blurted out that my husband had just died from Lupus and I just wanted them to know. A stunned couple stood at the literature rack getting help from the volunteer office manager whom I don't recall ever meeting. I turned to leave and go back to my car. It suddenly dawned on me that the poor couple had probably just received a diagnosis of Lupus and was there to gather information on how to cope. I'm sure I shook everyone up. That was totally not me! Was I going crazy?

More than once, I drove somewhere and do not recall how I got there or why I was at that particular location. My mind was so consumed with trying to accept the reality of Steve's death that I was not always aware of the present moment.

Once, I walked past a decorative mirror and caught a glimpse of a young woman's reflection. I was overcome with grief for her because she had just lost her husband. I had never felt such deep sorrow and compassion for a widow before. I burst into gut-wrenching tears for her…then I suddenly realized it was me!

For a while, I couldn't cry. I knew I should. There was no question of my deep love for Steve. Why would no tears come? I was beginning to think something was really wrong with me because I couldn't cry. Then one evening, I sat mindlessly watching some silly sitcom on TV. It was actually a funny show but my mind barely comprehended what was going on. Then a pet died in the show. It was supposed to be a funny situation, but I just broke down with wailing that would not stop. It was like a pent-up dam had gushed out and nothing could hold it back. It broke loose over a make believe pet's death! I must really be losing it!

Another thing that was very unlike me was to be so angry over little things- like seeing a couple holding hands while walking, or someone celebrating their fiftieth wedding anniversary (even those whom I truly loved!) Why did they still get to have their loved one and not me? Of course, I realized it was just the way it was. I also got extremely mad when I heard my friends get irritated with their husbands. Didn't they realize how precious their marriage and the time they had together were?

Then without warning, I would be filled with unexplainable joy! I felt a sudden urge to dance with unbridled happiness. It was the thought of Steve being completely free of all the pain and suffering I had to witness with no way to help him. I recall thinking others would never understand how I could experience joy in my grief.

The incredible range of emotions grief takes you through in such a short amount of time is enough to make anyone think they are going crazy. It's a roller-coaster journey through grief.

"There is a time for everything, and a season for every activity under heaven: a time to be born and a time to die, a time to plant and a time to uproot, a time to kill and a time to heal, a time to tear down and a time to build, a time to weep and a time to laugh, a time to mourn and a time to dance…" Ecclesiastes 3:1–4

Your Story- Am I Going Crazy?

(Write about some of your crazy emotions or thoughts)

_____

_____

_____

_____

_____

_____

_____

_____

_____

_____

_____

_____

_____

_____

_____

_____

_____

_____

_____

_____

_____

_____

_____

_____

_____

_____

_____

_____

_____

_____

_____

_____

_____

_____

_____

_____

_____

_____

_____

_____

_____

_____

_____

_____

_____

_____

_____

_____

_____

"And pray in the Spirit on all occasions with all kinds of prayers and requests." Ephesians 6:18

Helpful Input- Am I Going Crazy?

The crazy conflicting feelings you go through are one of the main things that tire you out so quickly. You may experience anger, sadness, fear, anxiety, happiness and deep hurt all within a matter of moments. Grief is hard work. You may not think you are doing much, but you may feel exhausted all the time. What used to be routine chores become huge mountains that seem impossible to scale. These are a few of the comments I've heard from grievers through the years:

"I'm afraid if I start crying, I will never stop."

The tears build up on the inside and will have to come out in some form sooner or later. They will not last forever. Research has actually proven that those deep wailing cries of grief actually contain healing stress toxins which cleanse your body of harmful chemicals. Tears of grief are made up of different substances than tears from irritants, for example. In other words, God designed tears to aide in our healing while grieving. That's why as much as you fight the tears, you feel better after a good cry.

> "Those who sow in tears will reap with songs of joy. He who goes out weeping, carrying seed to sow, will return with songs of joy, carrying sheaves with him." Psalm 126:5-6

"I can't concentrate on anything!"

While actively grieving, it is very challenging to focus on anything for very long. Your mind is consumed with remembering, reliving, reviewing and realizing all you are missing in your loved one. It requires the greater part of your energy and time right now. It won't always. Yet it does until you begin to adjust to your life without the one who was so important to you. It's difficult to be as productive as you were before. Your house may not stay as clean. Your car may not stay serviced. It's a real chore to keep the bills paid on time. Your mind might wander as you drive or try to watch a movie. Reading even becomes difficult as you work through the most challenging parts of your grief. Be gentle with yourself and give yourself time to grieve. You will begin to regain your focus as you hang on tight to the Lord and keep your eyes firmly fixed on Him through this painful time. He will lead you through.

> "In this you greatly rejoice, though now for a little while you may have had to suffer grief in all kinds of trials. These have come so that your faith- of greater worth than gold, which perishes even though refined by fire- may be proved genuine and may result in praise, glory and honor when Jesus Christ is revealed." 1 Peter1:6-7

"I don't believe I will ever be happy again."

It truly seems like all chance for happiness is gone. Many truly believe they will never smile again. In the depths of your sadness, it is almost impossible to think of ever experiencing true happiness again. You will. It may surprise you when you find yourself laughing or enjoying something. Some people feel guilty, or even disloyal, for feeling happy. It takes a while to let go of the pain. Your loved one doesn't want you to live in a constant state of sadness. For a while, it can be painful to see others celebrating and sharing life together. As you work through your grief, you will discover that the joy and happiness you begin to feel will be even richer than before. Happiness means much more to you after surviving the depths of grief. The time will eventually come when you want to cherish each moment and friendship much more deeply than before, because you realize it could be the last.

"You turned my wailing into dancing; You removed my sackcloth and clothed me with joy, that my heart may sing to You and not be silent. O Lord my God, I will give You thanks forever." Psalm 30:11-12

Practical Ideas- Am I Going Crazy?

"You will keep in perfect peace him whose mind is steadfast, because he trusts in You. Trust in the Lord forever, for the Lord, the Lord is the Rock eternal." Isaiah 26:3-4

- Write in a prayer journal daily. It will help keep you focused on the One who is Your faithful rock through this stormy season of your life.
- Listen to encouraging uplifting Christian music. It will also help keep your mind steadfast on the Lord, the only One who will never leave you.
- Be extra easy on yourself as you go through this time. Don't attempt too much at a time.
- When you get angry at someone else's happiness, turn it into a chance to be thankful for the special times you shared with your loved one. (Thankfulness keeps bitterness away)
- Give yourself permission to laugh at a joke, movie or conversation. Laughter is a great break from grief.
- Make a list of five things you are thankful for everyday (no repeats). You'll be surprised at how many things you can find to be thankful for even in the middle of your grief.
- Don't be afraid of crying spells. They relieve built up stress and actually heal your soul.
- Let your expectations of an immaculate house, finished projects, high production at work, and to keep everything running as usual relax a bit. Give yourself time and permission to grieve.
- Make sure to concentrate on driving safely because your mind will want to wander. Pull over if a big wave of grief comes over you while driving. Ride it out before driving on.
- It's OK to smile sometimes even when you don't feel like it. Your feelings will catch up to your face.
- Choose wisely who you want to vent your volatile emotions to. In the midst of your grief, you may say things that you might not really mean. God is the greatest listener. He knows you just need to talk and won't hold it against you. I've listened to many crazy statements without much comment because it was *just the grief talking.*
- Another reminder: Try not to make vital decisions which will affect your future while in a state of grief. It will not be made with your best judgement. (Whether to sell your house, car, remarry...)

"I am still confident of this: I will see the goodness of the Lord in the land of the living. Wait for the Lord; be strong and take heart and wait for the Lord." Psalm 27:13-14

Interactive Work page- Am I Going Crazy?

"Do not conform any longer to the pattern of this world, but be transformed by the renewing of your mind. Then you will be able to test and approve what God's will is- His good, pleasing and perfect will." Romans 12:2

- What specific ways am I afraid of going crazy or losing my mind?

  _____

  _____

- List decisions that I commit to holding off on decision until I am in a better state of mind?

  _____

  _____

- Who can I talk to who won't judge me for voicing crazy thoughts?

  _____

  _____

- How can I hold on to God, my Rock, through this turbulent time?

  _____

  _____

- Do I trust the Lord to walk with me through the Valley of the shadow of death and bring me out to the other side?

  _____

  _____

- Do the Lord and my loved one want me to experience peace and happiness again?

  _____

  _____

Jesus said in John 10:10b: "I have come that they may have life, and have it to the full."

Prayer Journal- Am I Going Crazy?

"Come to Me. All you who are weary and burdened and I will give you rest. Take My yoke upon you and learn from Me, for I am gentle and humble in heart, and you will find rest for your souls. For My yoke is easy and My burden is light."
Matthew 11:28-30

My Prayer Journal- Am I Going Crazy?

(note: your prayer journal will sound completely different than mine. You have different emotions, issues and situations to pray through.)

Heavenly Father,

All these crazy emotions keep swirling around me. There are times it seems out of control. I know where to run- to You! No one else knows how I truly feel. I don't even know how to feel! You are so patient with me as I try to muddle through Steve's death.

Sometimes I am driving and I hear a siren. I am immediately transported to one of the many traumatic times Steve was taken by ambulance as they fought for his life. It's like I am right back in that moment reliving all the emotions. I've been told these flashbacks won't last forever but it seems I'll never be the same. I often have to pull over until the trauma eases.

Sometimes I hear a song that takes me right to his side again- with all the love and closeness we ever felt. I swear I wake up hearing him strum his guitar at night. Guess I'm dreaming.

There are mornings I wake up after a night of grieving. The minute my mind wakes, the pain is fresh all over again as I realize Steve is really gone. I sure was hoping it was a dream. For a while it seemed like it was happening to someone else...or like I was watching a movie.

Yet it's real, isn't it, Lord! It helps me to think he is with you and he is free from suffering. But I sure could use him here. The kids need him. I need him. He was our strength. Now, I'm going to have to lean on You, Lord- more than ever before! Steve and I always talked about everything and figured out together how to handle each hurdle. The hurdles keep coming, Lord. I need You to help me figure things out.

Everyone has been incredibly kind. They realize I am a young widow with 4 children to raise. Someone started a fund to help us through this time. Although I am very grateful...at the same time, I'm very angry! Where was this help when we fought through the past 4 years of his illness? I don't want the money! I want Steve! I want the kids to have their dad! Money won't bring him back. I will gratefully accept these gifts because I know they've been given with love for us and for Steve. It's just these conflicting emotions that all struggle against one another all the time.

Sometimes I'm shocked at those friends I thought would be there for us—who are not. Perhaps it is more than they can handle. Maybe they just don't know what to do or say. It could be they have too much going on in their own life. Lord, I know I can count on You to never leave us or forsake us.

I cannot count on other people. I need to count on You. I cannot count on anyone to come and take Steve's place for no one could. There will never be another Steve. The kids, however, need to know they can count on me. Father, I ask You to be the father to our children and a husband to me. Lead our family. Help us through this time. Don't let my family fall apart! We need You, Lord!

I've been trying to be the dad to my kids, but I cannot. My older son is at the age, he needs a man show him how to be a man. I know You will guide him. My daughter is at such a critical age to lose her dad. She is turning into a young woman, almost ready to date. She needs her dad to show her what a good man looks like. She needs Your love. My 7 year old son lost his best buddy. He and his daddy watched movies together, collected pocket knives together and hung out together even in the midst of hospital stays. He needs Your comfort. My youngest son is only two years old. He needs his daddy. He needs You, Lord!

I need a protector, companion, lover, friend, provider, partner, guide…Lord, I know You will fill that role more and more as the void of Steve's presence becomes more and more obvious. As the craziness of grief threatens to envelope me and my children, I ask that You lead us through. May we rely on You more than we ever have before. You are our eternal Rock!

> *"Do not be afraid; you will not suffer shame. Do not fear disgrace; you will not be humiliated. You will forget the shame of your youth and remember no more the reproach of your widowhood. For your Maker is your husband- the Lord Almighty is His name- the Holy One of Israel is your Redeemer; He is called the God of all the earth."*
> *Isaiah 54:4-5*

Your Prayer Journal- Am I Going Crazy?

(Ask God to help you through the craziness of your grief.)

_____

_____

_____

_____

_____

_____

_____

_____

_____

_____

_____

_____

_____

_____

_____

_____

_____

_____

_____

_____

_____

_____

_____

_____

_____

_____
_____
_____
_____
_____
_____
_____
_____
_____
_____
_____
_____
_____
_____
_____
_____
_____
_____
_____
_____
_____
_____
_____
_____

"A father to the fatherless, a defender of widows, is God in His holy dwelling. God sets the lonely in families…" Psalm 68:5-6a

4

Those Painful Firsts

"Hear my prayer, O Lord; let my cry for help come to You. Do not hide Your face from me when I am in distress. Turn Your ear to me; when I call, answer me quickly." Psalm 102:1-2

Sharing Our Experiences:

EVERYTHING IN YOUR life has suddenly become divided by the time before and after your loved one's death. The first year, everything will be a first: the first month, birthday, anniversary...

My Story- Those Painful Firsts

The initial "first" that sticks out in my mind was my thirty-sixth birthday (just two weeks) after Steve's death. I know my family meant well. They organized a birthday party at a nearby restaurant. I was adamant. I didn't want to have a party; I never wanted to celebrate again! I certainly didn't want to think of growing another year older without my love by my side. There just wasn't enough strength to fight them. I somehow realized they needed it more than I did. My kids probably needed it as well. I surely didn't have it in me to even think about a birthday. I must have driven my children there to meet the rest of the family. I sat motionless and emotionless through the entire meal—not wanting to be there, but having nowhere else to go either. It might have appeared to be a regular family gathering, except the guest of honor (me) was not really there. The rest of the family probably talked to my kids. My mind was jumping through hoops—being mad that no one cared that I didn't want to celebrate; thinking that Steve would have understood my feelings; missing the one who had always made my birthday special; not believing it had been over two weeks since he died; mad that I would have to go through many more birthdays without him. Somehow I made it through and we went back home with gifts in tow. I didn't even remember opening them..

Right about that time, my eighth-grade daughter was up for Wrestling Queen. Her daddy had never seen her dressed in a formal dress complete with her hair fixed, jewelry and makeup. It broke my heart to see her looking so beautiful and grown up. They announced the parents of all the candidates, including her late dad's name. How I missed him sitting next to me for this moment! My heart was broken for me and for my daughter. He would miss so much more- her graduation, engagement, and marriage.

Then there came Valentine's Day, Mothers' Day and Father's day – all without my love.

About 6 months after his death, I faced my first crisis without Steve. I was washing dishes when the phone rang. My sister-in-law told me my seventeen-year old son, who worked for them, had been in a bad accident. He was unloading construction material in the back of a semi-truck when a huge load fell on top, trapping him underneath. Several men had tried with all their might to pull the heavy material off of him but couldn't. My brother jumped in full of extra adrenaline and lifted it off by himself. My son was being taken to get checked out. It appeared he had a broken wrist for sure. They weren't certain of other injuries. After getting someone to cover the kids, I drove as fast as I could to meet him at the Emergency Clinic. He had to undergo surgery and therapy. Afterward God used this injury to help partially pay for my son's college through a disability program.

As painful as all those first holidays, birthdays, and anniversaries were, we made it through each one—one at a time with God's faithful help. Every time a "first" approached, anxiety built. I had no idea how I could possibly face it without Steve- yet each time I discovered that the Lord was truly with me, helping me through. As each "first" came and went, I found I survived…and that I was not alone. God Almighty was there and would never ever leave me.

After over 20 years of that initial year of "firsts," there still continues to be other occasional "firsts" that I think of Steve and how much he would enjoy being a part of…like the birth of grandchildren and even the writing of this book. Yet somehow, I know he is very much a part of it!

"I will walk among you and be your God, and you will be My people." Leviticus26:12

Your Story- Those Painful Firsts

(Use this space to write about the "firsts" you have already faced without your loved one and those you fear facing in your future)

_____

_____

_____

_____

_____

_____

_____

_____

_____

_____

_____

_____

_____

_____

_____

_____

_____

_____

_____

_____

_____

_____

_____

_____
_____
_____
_____
_____
_____
_____
_____
_____
_____
_____
_____
_____
_____
_____
_____
_____
_____
_____
_____
_____
_____
_____

"Trust in the Lord with all your heart and lean not on your own understanding; in all your ways acknowledge Him, and He will make your paths straight." Proverbs 3:5-6

Helpful Input- Those Painful Firsts!

The whole first year without your loved one is filled with "firsts." It is your first time to face so many different occasions without your loved one by your side. The year is filled with holidays and special celebrations. I almost don't want to list them because you do well to handle one "first" at a time. Not only are there all the major holidays, but there are birthdays and anniversaries.

There are also plenty of surprise "firsts" like the initial time you have to get your oil changed, or school starts again, or the washing machine quits. Your loved one might have always taken care of certain things before that you are now forced to deal with. Or everyone else's child is starting back to school but yours won't ever again.

Don't try to face a whole year of facing "firsts" all at once. It is too much. It can be too overwhelming to think about the rest of your life without them as well. It's best to face each day as it comes. You can, however, plan ahead a bit for some of the special days coming up that you know will be extra hard. You might not be able to control the surprises that spring up, but it does help to plan for a special occasion—a few days to a week prior.

Most people find the anticipation and trepidation of a forthcoming day is often much worse than the actual day itself. So be aware that anxiety might rear its fearful head as the day approaches. Instead of giving in to dread, make a few simple plans to honor your loved one in a fitting way. If Mother's Day is coming up and you have lost a mom or a child, it can be overwhelming to think of all the Mother's Day cards and gifts people will be giving and receiving. It's all a harsh reminder of who you've lost. You walk down the aisle of the grocery store or mall, and there are Mother's Day signs everywhere. Songs, videos, commercials, movie—all focused on mothers. They even recognize moms at church. It can be extremely painful. Especially the first time!

It really helps to have some kind of simple plan for that day. Perhaps taking a Mother's Day gift to the grave; maybe watching a movie with another relative; planting some flowers in her garden; giving another mom or child a gift in honor of your loved one; going to eat with a friend; taking a walk with a grandchild. In other words, whatever the occasion is, orchestrate some way to honor the special relationship you had with your loved one.

Try your best to turn it into celebrating all the ways you are thankful for the relationship you had with your loved one instead of thinking of all you will be missing. Of course, you have to grieve what you are missing. That's what grief is. You are not grieving for your loved one, who no longer has to face the trials of this life; you grieve for yourself and the great void left in your life. But it helps to realize how blessed you have been to have them however long it was for.

With each "first" you make it through, there's a little bit more assurance you can make it through this painful process called grief

A few of the other "firsts" that can hit hard are the first time the headstone is set in the ground. There's something about seeing your loved one's name and date of death in stone that makes it so much more real than ever before. Just expect that. You don't always get told ahead of time. Many people have gone to visit the grave site and have been blind-sided by the sight. If it hasn't been set yet, perhaps you can ask them to notify you ahead of tiem. Take extra time (and tissues) to sit and take it in.

Another milestone in the first year is making to the anniversary of their death. Even though you might have come a long way in healing, there's something about it being a full year that hits hard. You can barely believe a whole year has gone by without them. Most people report kind of a review of their grief and pain as they reach the first year mark. It lessens the blow to mark this date with some kind of activity with a friend or family.

There are a lot of "firsts" to get through without your loved one. It's true, you do have to learn to go on without them. It definitely takes time and work; but it also helps to think of another important "first." That will be the first time you see them again when your journey here is through—when it is time to take your first step into heaven—when you will never have to say goodbye again.

"When you pass through the waters, I will be with you; and when you pass through the rivers, they will not sweep over you. When you walk through the fire, you will not be burned; the flames will not set you ablaze. For I am the Lord, your God, the Holy One of Israel, your Savior…" Isaiah 43:2–3

Practical Ideas- Those Painful Firsts

"When He saw her weeping, and the Jews who had come along with her also weeping, He was deeply moved in spirit and troubled. 'Where have you laid him?' He asked. 'Come and see, Lord,' they replied. JESUS WEPT." John 11:33–35

Although Jesus knew He would resurrect Lazarus from the dead, He wept. He wept at the grief He saw them going through. You have a Lord who understands your grief and cries for you. Yet He also died to give you a choice to have eternal life with Him.

- Although you may want some alone time, try not to be isolated by yourself all day on one of these "firsts."
- Write in this book or in a prayer journal on one of your *first* days.
- For their birthday or another occasion, get a gift you know they would like and give it to someone in need, or someone in the family who will cherish it.
- In honor of their birthday/other occasion give one of their special belongings to someone who will appreciate it.
- Make their favorite dessert/meal and share it with another
- Give a big stuffed animal to a child in their honor
- Be creative. A man who had done a lot of work on our church's computers had a vision of an open wifi for all to use who were in the church building. Someone set this up and made the password his name. What a great memorial for one who had helped so many with their computers.
- When my son and daughter-in-law got married, they displayed a portrait of Steve in front where the family sits, to honor all he meant to them.
- My mom often reads a letter written by my dad at our Christmas gatherings
- Hang a special ornament at Christmas (some are made with a place for a photo)
- Write a letter to your loved one
- Make a list of ways you are thankful for having them in your life

"May God, the source of hope, fill you with joy and peace through your faith in Him. Then you will overflow with hope by the power of the Holy Spirit." Romans 15:13

Interactive Work page- Those Painful Firsts

"He (Jesus) was a man of sorrows and acquainted with grief...Surely our griefs He Himself bore, and our sorrows He carried." Isaiah 53:3,4

- List some of the "firsts" you know you will need to face:

_____

_____

- Do not try to face any of your *firsts* alone. Tell God right now what the *first* is that you are dreading. Ask His help:

_____

_____

- What are some ideas you can think of to honor your loved one on that day?

_____

_____

- Who do you want to share that day with?

_____

_____

- Why will that day be especially hard for you?

_____

_____

"He is the healer of the brokenhearted. He is the one who bandages their wounds." Psalm 147:3

Prayer Journal- Those Painful Firsts

"Hear, O Lord, and be gracious to me; O Lord, be my helper. You have turned for me my mourning into dancing." Psalm 30:10-11

My Prayer Journal- Those Painful Firsts

(Remember, these are excerpts from my prayer journals. Many days my prayers repeated the same thing over or rambled. God still heard and led me through—just as He will you)

Heavenly Father,

Every day there are more things I have to face without my love by my side. I walked out to the mailbox to bring our mail inside. An older gentleman who lives in the neighborhood was walking and stopped to talk to me. He had heard about Steve's recent death and offered his sympathy. Then I heard these words for the first time, "You're young. You will marry again!" I was so mad I literally wanted to punch him in the face. I don't believe I've ever been so mad. The depth of my anger shocked me. (The well-meaning neighbor never knew my fury, but I sure felt it!) Father, I never want to marry again! How can anyone ever replace Steve? There will never be another man who could possibly love me and know me like Steve. He has spoiled me for all other men…Even the thought made me furious, yet I do not want to go through life with such vicious anger. I don't even want to be bitter. Father, help me think instead of all the sweet memories we've shared. Most people never get to experience the love we shared together. Help me not hold it against this gentleman. He truly meant well. Sometimes people say the worst possible things at the most inopportune time.

****

I didn't think it would be so painful to walk into church the first time! There was the row where we always sat together. In front was the altar we stood at when we exchanged marriage vows. This was the seat I wanted to slide down and hide under when Steve announced we were expecting our youngest (our surprise!) He was so proud I thought he would explode! I was embarrassed and in total shock. How could I have another baby! We already knew Steve was dying. We were already under severe financial pressure. What would people think? What did I think?! Yet this new expected baby gave Steve a new lease on life. He was determined to live long enough for his son to remember him! Now that baby is two years old and in the nursery down the hall. What a stab in the heart to sit down without my wonderful husband at this church where we shared so much history. Yet, I needed to be there even if it was hard. I needed the reassurance of heaven and eternal life. The songs, scripture and spoken words all were tender reminders from You that Steve is alive and better than ever; that the kids and I will be OK. Even if I don't feel OK, I know I can hold on tight to You and Your promises, Lord. I know You are holding me.

******

Lord, that first Thanksgiving was incredibly harder than I expected. It was the first major holiday with Steve's family who loved to cook and eat. I felt very much a part of his family after 18 years of marriage plus 4 years of dating. I was so glad to be with them. It was like still getting to be a part of Steve. I know the kids were happy to be there, as well. It all was going well until a country musician on TV started singing, "I'm so lonesome I could die." I completely broke down without a moment's warning. The tears came so hard, I really thought I might die. There was something about being with his family that hit me. Things would never be the same. Though they were all so supportive, yet Steve wasn't there. And he never would be again. Although it was 10 months after his death, it hit me like it was fresh grief all over again…for he would never be a part of these family holiday gatherings again. Each first is a brand new reason to grieve because he won't be part of that occasion again. Father, I'm just so glad You are always with me…for all eternity… You are my first and my last love. Thank You for patiently showing me this through all these firsts I've had to go through.

"Do not grieve for the joy of the Lord is your strength." Nehemiah 8:10b

Your Prayer Journal- Those Painful Firsts

(Bring your burdens of your "firsts" to the Lord by writing in your prayer journal here.)

_____

_____

_____

_____

_____

_____

_____

_____

_____

_____

_____

_____

_____

_____

_____

_____

_____

_____

_____

_____

_____

_____

_____

_____

_____

_____

_____
_____
_____
_____
_____
_____
_____
_____
_____
_____
_____
_____
_____
_____
_____
_____
_____
_____
_____
_____
_____
_____
_____
_____

"Praise be to the Lord, to God our Savior, who daily bears our burdens. " Psalm 68:18

Remember When

"The memory of the righteous will be a blessing…" Proverbs 10:7a

Sharing Our Experiences:

ONE OF THE major tasks of grief is to look back over the unique relationship we had with our loved one. That includes reviewing all the memories we shared. It helps us more fully appreciate the love we shared.

My Story- Remember When

When Steve first died, it was hard to get past the trauma of his illness and death. The numerous ambulance rides, hospital stays, and Intensive Care visits kept flashing before me, transporting me back into those critical moments. Crisis upon crisis helped kept me from having time to process one situation before the next screamed into our lives. It was like 4 years of straight trauma. At the same time, I was trying to create a normal family life and maintain a loving licensed child care home. Our teenagers were trying to build their own lives with friends and experiences. The younger two needed stability. I needed God's help to work through all the emotional minefields we had just come through so I could keep my family together since Steve's death.

In some ways, it seemed like much of that trauma began pouring back in the first few weeks after

Steve's death. I would be driving and see an ambulance in route to the hospital. I would have to pull over until I calmed down. It seemed like I was reliving one of Steve's episodes—like it was happening in that moment. If I went to visit someone in the hospital, it seemed the hardest thing in the world was to go through those doors (sometimes the very same doors I had gone through so many times before to be with Steve). Watching TV was almost impossible when hospital scenes came on. Scenes would pop into my mind with Steve during times of severe suffering—when I could do nothing to help him. I wondered if I would ever get through all the painful memories surrounding his illness and death.

One night several weeks after his death, I dreamed of him. The first part of the dream he appeared old and frail, walking with a cane. (Even though he was only 37 years old at the time of his death, he often had to use oxygen and a cane.) As the dream went on, I was shocked because he suddenly appeared glowing with health and peace. I was thrilled for him to be healed and free from suffering. That seemed to be a turning point for my memories. The painful scenes of suffering and death still came—yet less frequently—and the beautiful memories started flowing:

Steve was the cashier at our local neighborhood grocery store. He checked me out as I bought a cake mix on my fifteenth birthday. Later that night, he got my phone number from a friend and started calling me every night. That was the first time our lives merged with millions more memories to follow… country rides on the back of his motorcycle with summer breezes caressing our faces…fishing at the lake…surprise flowers delivered…movies with friends…proms…his graduation…almost breaking up… getting engaged…my graduation…our long-awaited wedding…our first little apartment…his baptism… fixing up our first house…preparing for a baby…sewing matching flannel shirts for Steve and our newborn son…little baby girl and daddy- both sick enough to be in the hospital at the same time… business started…country living…Steve's brother's suicide…another baby full of hope…business failed/ loss of all we built—but more love than ever…Steve's writing and music…songwriting and guitar music filling our lives…increasing sickness/falls…hospital stays…coming to term with his approaching death… surprise pregnancy…Steve's determination to live longer…crazy family vacation with kids, meds and oxygen in tow...pontoon boat with waves crashing in sudden storm…rush back to city to the hospital with pneumonia…birth of our surprise baby…Steve died in my arms/brought back/ put on life support… finally home health care…at home with family…sweet last year…even more precious last night…

Steve's illness and death were a huge part of my memory of him, yet there have been so many other priceless parts of our lives together. The painful memories pale in comparison to the beautiful life moments we shared together. As I consider all the blessings we have shared, I have become more and more thankful for the precious memories that remain part of me forever.

"I thank God every time I remember you." Philippians 1:3

Your Story- Remember When

(Write about the life you shared with your loved one. Use whatever form seems best for you. It can be random thoughts, a list of moments, or your whole history in story form. Even if your writing doesn't make sense to anyone else, you know what those words mean to you. You might have scenes play in your mind, feelings well up in your heart or thoughts tie together as you go back through your memories. You may sob, laugh, become angry or sad. It's all part of reviewing the significance of your relationship. It's part of working through grief)

_____

_____

_____

_____

_____

_____

_____

_____

_____

_____

_____

_____

_____

_____

_____

_____

_____

_____

_____

_____

_____

_____

_____

_____

_____

_____

_____

_____

_____

_____

_____

_____

_____

_____

_____

_____

_____

_____

_____

_____

_____

"May the Lord keep watch between you and me when we are away from each other."
Genesis 31:49b

Helpful Input- Remember When

One of the most important things that needs to happen after the death of a loved one is for you to go back over their life and realize how much they impacted you. A lot of people think if they avoid thinking of their loved one, or reviewing their memories, they might be able to avoid the pain. In reality, as you go back through memories you shared with your loved one, you will begin to be thankful for the times and love you shared (no matter how short). You are able to come to peace with the beauty of the special bond you had and find rich blessings in that.

It is true, there will be pain involved as you reminisce. Tears will probably flow. Some of those tears will be deep gut-wrenching wails. As noted before, tears of grief have a different enzyme which aides in healing. God designed our bodies to produce those healing tears at the right time. Someone who went through my grief support group once said, tears are love spilling out. Don't be afraid of the tears. Let them flow. You can even set aside a time to go over memories either alone or with another family member or friend.

Of course, not everyone cries. Don't be concerned if you don't have tears for a while. That happens as well. Some people just do not cry. Then again, sometimes the dam breaks when you least expect it. Everyone has different personalities, unique relationships and their own way of dealing with grief.

It is tempting to use something to numb the pain- like medication, drugs, alcohol or food. In the years of helping people see they can make it through their time of deep loss, I have seen medications passed out far too easily. There are times antidepressants and sleeping pills may truly be necessary. For the most part, the best way to go through the pain is to go through it. As a woman goes through labor, she endures pain for a while, but in the end new life comes. The same will happen for you when you hold the Lord's hand as you go through your painful loss.

There are plenty of other ways besides medication to avoid the pain of memories. Some people take shopping to a whole new level—especially if there is life insurance money available. Buying something new can be exciting and take the edge off your pain for a while—until the bills start coming. Far too many grievers have ended up with a mountain of debt to deal with, along with the grief they still need to go through. Others immediately try to run away through travel or moving to a new home to escape any memories. At some point, you still have to come home or face the loss in some way.

Some people are tempted to jump right into another relationship to try to fill the excruciating void. The problem is they can jump into a relationship that is harmful, or one they are definitely not ready for. Try not to be afraid of being alone long enough to come to terms with the deep loss of this relationship before jumping into another. It's not fair to you or to the other person. If you will use this time to deepen you relationship with the Lord, who never leaves you or forsakes you, you will have so much more to share with another person when the time is right. You will also have better discernment after the rawness begins to heal. You will also gain all the new wisdom from going through the grief, and from reviewing your relationship with your loved one.

Some people avoid their pain through excessive work, staying busy with all kinds of activities—anything that will help them deny the pain they might feel. Others try to escape through excessive entertainment, extreme exercise, and sex. Those things are not completely bad unless they are used in the wrong way. If they are being used as a way to avoid the journey through grief, it's just delaying or sometimes compounding grief. It's much more natural and healthy to approach the painful feelings as something that needs to be gone through as you deal with your loved one's loss. It will not last forever –especially at the initial intensity (unless it is avoided).

It is perfectly healthy to take breaks from grief; to watch a movie, have dinner, or to go shopping. Grieving is hard work and takes a toll on you physically, mentally and spiritually. You have been wounded and need to be gentle with yourself as you recover.

Going through memories is a vital part of healthy grieving. As you take a walk back through the life you shared, you are able to go forward carrying the very best parts of your loved one with you. Life will be sweeter because of all you shared. Go ahead and grieve, but with the hope that the Lord is with you and has blessed you with precious memories of your loved one.

"I have loved you with an everlasting love; I have drawn you with loving-kindness. I will build you up again and you will be rebuilt…" Isaiah 31:3b-4a

Practical Ideas- Remember When

"…a righteous man will be remembered forever." Psalm 112:6

- Expect tears and memories to flow. Instead of doing everything you can to avoid them, lean into them. You can even set aside a certain time specifically to go through memories. You will realize how blessed you are to have your loved one in your life.
- Create a photo album of some of the special pictures When you are ready to go through some of their personal belongings, share stories and memories those items bring up.
- When you give an item away, tell the person receiving it a memory that goes along with that object. Not only does it pass along history, it makes that article of furniture, clothing, or tool much more valuable to the receiver.

- When a sight, sound or smell sets off memories of your loved one, stop and share it with someone. It's like sharing a story of your love.
- When you face a certain situation, think of how your loved one would have handled it. That's not to say, that has to be how you take care of the situation. But sometimes, their strengths in life continue to help you.
- Laugh at a funny show you watched together.
- Try not to fear the varied emotions your memories will take you through (sadness, joy, anger, fear, loneliness, irritation, hilarity...) The deep sentiments you experience as you grieve the loss of your loved one's companionship will actually work together to help you through this time.
- Reviewing the life you shared with your loved one will help you take the best parts forward.
- Concentrate on the blessings you shared, not on all you are missing.

"Remember the wonders He has done, His miracles, and the judgements He pronounced."
1 Chronicles 16:12

Interactive Work page- Remember When...

"How can we thank God enough for you in return for all the joy we have in the presence of our God because of you?" 1 Thessalonians 3:9

- List some of the fun moments you shared with your loved one:

  _____

  _____

- Tell of some of the best places you were able to go together:

  _____

  _____

- What are some of the biggest blessings that came from your relation?

  _____

  _____

- Write down the hardest things you faced together...

  _____

  _____

- Tell which activities you enjoyed sharing with your loved one-

  _____

  _____

- How did your relationship change from when you first met until now?

  _____

  _____

"Do not be anxious about anything, but in everything, by prayer and petition, with thanksgiving, present your requests to God. And the peace of God, which transcends all understanding, will guard your hearts and your minds in Christ Jesus." Philippians 4:6-7

My Prayer Journal- Remember When…

"Hear my prayer, O Lord; let my cry for help come to You. Do not hide Your face from me when I am in distress. Turn Your ear to me; when I call, answer me quickly." Psalm 102:1-2

Heavenly Father,

I often feel as though my life is over and will never be the same without Steve by my side. The pit of despair and self-pity is trying to pull me down. Tonight as I was slipping into the darkness of sorrow, I remembered tiny little Miss Ola. She is a 84 year old widow who has been coming to our grief support group. She recently lost a son to death. However, she has also faced the loss of a baby, another daughter, her husband—and is now battling cancer throughout her body. Her daughter wheels her into our group along with her oxygen tank, and then comes back to pick her up when our group is over. Our group is full of people going through full-blown grief over the death of a loved one. Some have lost spouses, children or parents. The mood can be pretty painful at times. Yet Miss Ola (who has suffered more than all of us) always tells us that no matter what, we always need to count our blessings.

So, Lord, here goes! Even though I'm not feeling thankful at all right now, I'm going to follow Miss Ola's advice. I'm going to list my blessings:

I am thankful to have had Steve in my life for almost 18 years of marriage and 4 years of dating before that. I'm thankful for the deep love we've shared. Not everyone has the chance to love their soulmate so deeply for so long. I'm thankful for the moonlit walks, fishing on lazy summer days, listening to Steve's guitar playing and songs he wrote while I'm cooking. I'm so grateful for the hundreds of poems he penned, songs he wrote for every birthday and anniversary. I'm thankful for the children we've had together- Eric, our first, with his determination, self-control and fun sense of humor; Chrissy, our only daughter, with her bright smile, deep compassion and strong will; Ryan, your buddy, who has stayed close by your side all through his young years just to share time with his daddy while he can; Jake, our youngest and biggest surprise, who has brought immense joy, adventure and life in his short two years. Our children bring so many reasons to keep going and a love that deepens as they grow.

I'm thankful for the long action stories Steve used to tell the kids, using them as the main characters. I'm grateful for the joyful way he had for looking at life and making everyone feel welcome. There are so many fun adventures- hikes in the woods, impromptu road trips, treasure hunts, and vacations. I am so grateful for late night conversations, listening to music out under the stars, and learning to dance together.

I am thankful for the way we both desired to live for You, Lord. What a joy to share in our love for You, to serve You together, to see where You led each day. What a beautiful adventure You sent us on in this life together.

He's free! I'm so grateful that Steve is finally free of all pain and suffering. It was hard watching him and not being able to do anything. We prayed for healing, but You let him know that if he was willing to go through this, You would use his suffering to help many people. Lord, I can even say thank You for his willingness to go through the trauma and pain—trusting You to use it.

Thank You for never leaving us alone to face anything, but being with us every step of the way. You are so faithful, Lord. Our life together has been richly blessed—not by the world's standards, for we had medical bills far beyond our ability to pay. Yet we have always had You, Lord…and one another. Our love for You and for one another grew far beyond my wildest dreams. Thank You for the honor of sharing Steve's life.

Father, it is true, when we thank You, our hearts begin to overflow with gladness- even in the midst of grief.

> *"You turned my wailing into dancing; You removed my sackcloth and clothed me with joy, that my heart might sing to You and not be silent. O Lord, my God, I will give You thanks forever." Psalm 30:11-12*

Your Prayer Journal- Remember When...

"I will remember the deeds of the Lord; yes, I will remember Your miracles of long ago. I will meditate on all Your works and consider all Your mighty deeds." Psalm 77:11

(Even if you don't feel like it, begin to think of all the ways God has been with you as you shared life with your loved one. Thanking Him will draw you close to Him.)

_____

_____

_____

_____

_____

_____

_____

_____

_____

_____

_____

_____

_____

_____

_____

_____

_____

_____

_____
_____
_____
_____
_____
_____
_____
_____
_____
_____
_____
_____
_____
_____
_____
_____
_____
_____
_____
_____
_____
_____
_____
_____
_____
_____

"Give thanks to the Lord, for He is good. His love endures forever." Psalm 136:1

6

All Alone

"You have taken from me my closest friends and have made me repulsive to them. I am confined and cannot escape; my eyes are dim with grief. I call to You, O Lord, every day; I spread out my hands to You." Psalm 88:8-9

Sharing Our Experiences:

THIS IS A reminder that I share my story with you just so you'll know you are not alone; that others have endured grief before you and have survived. You grief will be completely different than mine because you are not me. Also, there will never be another one like your loved one and the relationship you shared together.

My Story- All Alone:

The first time I walked into my front door by myself, I had never felt such intense loneliness. My teenagers were with friends and the two younger boys were spending the evening watching a movie with family friends. It might have been the first time I had a whole evening to myself since Steve's death. It hit me as I put the key into the door. I was alone. Pulling the door open, I peered into our family home that had always held so much noise, activities and loving memories. The house had never been darker and more foreboding. I'm not sure how long it took me to get my nerve up to actually walk inside- alone. It seemed like forever.

Even turning on a few lights couldn't dispel the dark emptiness. There was no sound. I stood lost, not knowing what to do. Out of sheer habit, I walked towards the answering machine to check for messages. Nothing. I was overcome with the thought I would never again hear a message with my love's voice on it. There were no calls to check on me. No friendly voice. I was all alone in the world. Everyone else had a life but me. My life seemed to have stopped…and would never be happy.

My teenagers, even my younger boys had friends. My best friend, the love of my life, my life partner, my husband was gone. Life would never be the same. I was all alone in this world with no one who cared for me the way he did. Never had I felt so lonely in all my life.

My mind knew I had four children whom I loved—and who loved me. My house would be full of noise as soon as everyone was home—especially when all the children in my licensed childcare home came back Monday morning. My brain knew I had other family and friends who loved me… but the very core of my soul knew my Steve was gone and I was alone without him. In over 20 years, I had never had to face anything without my life partner, my other half. There was a loneliness no one else could reach.

I'm not certain how I finished out that evening of profound aloneness. Perhaps I cried myself to sleep. I might have called my earthly lifeline- Barbara, Steve's mom (my grieving partner). I know I wrote in my prayer journal- reaching out for dear life to the Lord. That could have been a slow transitioning point of turning to the One I already knew—Jesus. As much as Steve didn't want to leave me; he eventually had to. I would eventually come to discover that Jesus Christ would never ever leave me; that I would never be alone.

"Yes, I am with you always. You hold on to my right hand." Psalm 73:23

Your Story- All Alone:

> *"Even though I walk through the valley of the shadow of death, I will fear no evil, for You are with me." Psalm 23:4a*

(Write how loneliness has affected you since your loved one's death)

_____

_____

_____

_____

_____

_____

_____

_____

_____

_____

_____

_____

_____

_____

_____

_____

_____

_____

_____

_____

_____

_____

_____

_____

_____

_____

_____

_____

_____

_____

_____

_____

_____

_____

_____

_____

_____

_____

_____

_____

_____

_____

_____

_____

_____

"For there is no one who regards me; there is no escape for me; no one cares for my soul. I cried out to You, O Lord; I said, 'You are my refuge, My portion in the land of the living. Give heed to my cry, for I am brought very low.'" Psalm 142:4-6

Helpful Input- All Alone:

In my opinion, one of the hardest parts of grief is the terrible loneliness. We were designed to interact with and love others. When someone you love dies, it is easy to feel alone in the world. You will often feel intense loneliness even when you are surrounded by people. The deep ache of loneliness comes from being separated from your loved one, whether it was a spouse, child, parent or friend. You long for their companionship. Even if it wasn't the best relationship, you ache for what you hoped that relationship could have been. Loneliness can feel even deeper when it seems there is no one else to go through this grief with you.

Steve and I had done everything together. Because of his intense illness, it often seemed like it was "him and me" against the world. I always had him to bounce things off of. He was a huge part of my life- truly the other half of me. In fact, his illness had in many ways isolated us from the rest of the world. We had to withdraw from many activities and spend our time at home or in doctor offices or hospitals. Some of our best friends were doctors and nurses that I no longer saw after his death. There was no need. I knew I needed to make a concerted effort to reach out to others and build on existing relationships and make some new ones. But I also knew not to push it while I was in the depths of grieving.

In the middle of your grief, you probably need others more than ever. Yet many people tend to withdraw. There is need for support and friendship. Be careful who you reach out to when you're in a vulnerable state of grief. Build on a friendship you already have. Choose just a few trusted people you can confide in on a deeper level about your grief. A friend who is a great listener is a good starting place.

If you can find someone who will patiently listen while you tell what you are going through, you have found a treasure! You may need to repeat things as you work through your emotions. If you can find more than one confidante you can vent to, that divides the load between them. You won't always need the extra attention, but it's very helpful as you work through your grief. That's one nice thing about grief support groups. If you can find one you feel comfortable in, you will have a built-in group of people who are going through similar situations and will understand your need to talk or just listen.

It helps to take the initiative and don't wait for others to come to you. Many people have no idea what to say or do around someone grieving—so they tend to avoid you. They are afraid to talk about your loved one, for fear they will hurt you. Sometimes they even fear mentioning their name. They do not understand that's exactly what you need. You want to hear their precious name; that they were important to others; that their life matters. So open the door. Talk about your loved one—their life, their death, what you miss, their impact on your life, how you are doing. Set the cue so others will know you want and need to talk. If they say the wrong thing, try not to hold it against them. They are fumbling, trying to help.

Loneliness remains for a long time. It's often the most challenging issue to get through. As you work through your grief, a large share of effort is learning to cope without the physical presence of your loved one. You can get through this. You may not want to learn to live without them—but you can! With God's help, you will.

Some of the loneliest times may even be in the midst of a crowd where you miss your loved one the most: at church seeing others sit together; at family get-togethers where you loved one was always with you; during holiday celebrations, weddings, movies, at the mall—anywhere that reminds you how much you miss your loved one.

You won't always feel so lonely, but you can expect it for a while until you begin to heal. It will take time to work through the isolation you feel. In time, the Lord will help you build a new life (but you will never forget the old). You will experience joy again, and might even learn to enjoy quiet solitude.

My prayer for you: May you find in your deepest loneliness that you are never alone. May you find the very best friend you could ever have in Jesus Christ. He is with you in the darkest night, the brightest day, and for ever and ever. There is nothing that can separate you from His love.

> *"For I am convinced that neither death nor life, neither angels nor demons, neither the present nor the future, nor any powers, neither height nor depth, nor anything else in all creation, will be able to separate us from the love of God that is in Christ Jesus our Lord."*
> *Romans 8:38-39*

Practical Ideas- All Alone:

> *"Look to my right and see; no one is concerned for me. I have no refuge; no one cares for my life. I cry to You, O Lord; I say, 'You are my refuge, my portion in the land of the living.' Listen to my cry, for I am in desperate need…" Psalm 142:4-6a*

- Write in this journal when an attack of loneliness comes.
- Keep your friends' numbers in your cell phone for those attacks of loneliness
- Pray to the best friend you can ever have--your Lord God, who never gets tired of hearing your heart, and who is always available day and night.

- Get a pet to care for and keep you company.
- Invite someone to go somewhere with you.
- When loneliness attacks while in a group, let someone know how you feel—that you are missing your loved one.
- Build up an old friendship by doing more together.
- Deepen family relations—but don't depend on your kids to be your only friends.
- Put yourself in situations where you can make friends more easily. Go to church; join a bowling league; volunteer to work at a hospital or school. Don't expect new relationships to be as deep as the one you are grieving. Remember how much time, energy and history it took for that relationship to deepen.
- Take up a hobby: Fishing, knitting, piano, golf. Start a project, but go slow and easy. Don't expect to accomplish things at your usual speed for a while. There's more on limited brain capacity in the chapter, "Am I Going Crazy?"
- Attend a grief support group
- Help someone else. It will help you.
- Make friends with yourself. Use this time to get to know you better. You'll end up having more to share with others.
- Do something physical. Go for a walk. Ride a bike. Exercise. (Talk to God as you go!)
- Listen to music- encouraging is better than sad. Christian music focuses our hearts on the Lord.

"Turn to me and be gracious to me, for I am lonely and afflicted. Relieve the troubles of my heart and free me from my anguish." Psalm 25:16-17

Interactive Work page- All Alone

Grief takes a lot of work to get through. You can take an active role in your recovery. Some days will seem a lot better than others. Sometimes while grieving, your mind doesn't function too well, so here's a list you can refer to when the loneliness of grief threatens to overwhelm you.

- People I can call (list their phone numbers in your cell phone as well as here)

_____

_____

- Places I'd like to go:

_____

_____

- Music I like to listen to:

_____

_____

- Hobbies I would like to start (Take it slow and don't expect too much):

_____

_____

- Movies I might want to see or books I might want to read:

_____

_____

- Physical activities I enjoy:

_____

_____

- Friendships I would like to deepen:

_____

_____

- Possible new friendships:

_____

_____

"Don't be afraid; because I am with you. Don't be intimidated; I am your God. I will strengthen you. I will help you. I will support you with my victorious right hand." Isaiah 41:10

Prayer Journal- Loneliness:

"Be strong and courageous. Do not be terrified; do not be discouraged, for the Lord your God will be with you wherever you go." Joshua 1:9

My Prayer Journal:

Father,

I feel all alone in this world. I miss Steve so much. How can I go on without him? Father, please help me! I can't handle this awful loneliness by myself. Life seems so empty without him here. I know he can't come back. Everything seems so scary, unstable and hollow without him here. Show me how to go on. I just can't make it on my own.

I miss his warmth, his touch, his voice, his laugh, his hugs, his smiling eyes. I long for his company. There is a deep void where he used to be, and I fear I will drown in it. I miss sharing little things with him. I just want to talk to him and be with him once more.

Father, I don't think I can stand to be this lonely for the rest of my life! I know I have to go on without him, but I don't know how. Please be with me, Father, Help me adjust to his absence. Be my friend, my comforter, my safe place. You love me even more than Steve ever could. Help me really believe that, and to rest in Your arms right now. You are the only one who truly understands the fear and pain I feel right now. Help me through this, Father!

You are the only one who doesn't change or leave. Your love is always surrounding me. Hold me, Lord—for I can't stand on my own. Jesus, You are my Savior. Thank You for saving me from this deep abyss of loneliness and self-pity which threatens to drown me. You are my life-line! Help me hold tight to Your loving hand through this grief. I know I can make it through with You.

Help me handle this season of loneliness with grace and honor, the way You want me to. I know there is a purpose for all things. You can use this in my life for good. Help me submit to Your will even through this loneliness.

Father, Let me use this time to draw closer to You. Help me know that I will find everything I need in You. Thank You for being my best Friend and the greatest love of my life. Help me reach out to others. When I begin feeling sorry for myself, help me remember I'm not the only person in the world. Give me the courage I need to reach out to others. I need their friendship and they need mine. Help me remember it will take time to build new friendships and that I will never have another exactly like the one I have with Steve. But, I can pass on love to others more fully because of the love we've shared together. Father, let my love for others be a tribute to Your love and to Steve's love.

Thank You, Lord, for the gift of love You gave Steve and me together. Help me learn to go on without him here. Teach me to live in his absence. Help me get to know You better, Father. When I draw close to You; I am drawing closer to Steve—for he is with You now.

Father, I know my separation from Steve will not be forever. Someday, I will be with You both. We will live eternally in Your Holy presence. What a wonderful day that will be! Lord, however long I have left in this life, help me stay close to You. Let me know what You want me to do with the rest of my life. Help me reach out to other people with Your love. Thank You, Father, for staying with me and never leaving me alone. You are my strength and my life. Amen.

"A father to the fatherless, a defender of widows, is God in his holy dwelling. God sets the lonely in families…" Psalm 68:5-6

Your Prayer Journal- Loneliness:

> *"Be strong and courageous. Do not be afraid or terrified because of them, for the Lord your God goes with you; he will never leave you nor forsake you." Deuteronomy 31:6*

(Write your prayer to God about your loneliness or whatever else you are feeling. Be honest with your emotions. Pour yourself out to Him. He listens past the awkward words to your very heart!)

_____

_____

_____

_____

_____

_____

_____

_____

_____

_____

_____

_____

_____

_____

_____

_____

_____

_____

_____

_____

_____

_____
_____
_____
_____
_____
_____
_____
_____
_____
_____
_____
_____
_____
_____
_____
_____
_____
_____
_____
_____
_____
_____
_____
_____
_____
_____
_____
_____

Jesus said, … "And remember that I am always with you until the end of time."
Matthew 28:20

Helping Children Grieve

"Jesus said, 'Let the little children come to Me, and do not hinder them, for the kingdom of heaven belongs to such as these.' When He placed His hands on them, He went on from there." Matthew 19:14-15

Sharing Our Experiences:

I FELT LED to add this chapter because many times people are so caught up in their own grief, they forget (or do not know how) to help children grieve. Perhaps you don't have children who are grieving the loss of your loved one. Yet there could be young friends or relatives who are affected. Don't forget the kids. The children's version of MY FOREVER MEMORIES OF YOU is a MEMORY BOOK TO help children and youth work through their grief

.

My Story- Helping Children Grieve

I hurt just as badly for my children as for myself after Steve's death. As broken and hurt as I was without my husband, I knew my children were devastated by their dad's death. I recall when I was five years old, my little newborn baby brother died after living three days. Because we lived in a small town, my brothers and I were split up to stay with friends and family. My dad had to go with the ambulance to take my tiny brother to a larger city hospital better equipped to save his life. Mom had to stay in the hospital for two weeks due to complications so she didn't even get to attend our baby's funeral. Dad was overwhelmed with facing this tragedy without my mom. I recall walking into the service as a little girl, seeing my little baby brother for the first time in a tiny casket—with no one to explain what happened. By the time my mom came home, she had missed the rest of her children so much; she was thrilled to see us. I couldn't understand how someone could be so happy when our little baby died. I don't recall anyone talking to me about his death. Now that my children faced the death of their dad, I wanted to be sure to help them in any way I could.

Of course, each of my children was at a different stage in their life. They each had their own personal relationship with their dad which affected the way they each grieved. My oldest was 17 years old, approaching manhood. I didn't know until later that his dad had told him he might have to quit his much-loved basketball to work more hours to help me out. (He was already working and going to school.) Other well-meaning people told him he would need to be the man of the house now. The day of the funeral, Eric brought in the mail and was going through it. When I asked what he was doing, he said he had to figure out how to pay the bills. I told him that was my job. His was to finish school. He feared I would not be able to handle his dad's death and felt helpless when he saw me crying. I had to reassure him I would be fine…that I just needed to grieve.

Our only daughter, Chrissy, was fifteen and had always been a daddy's girl. They had fun together until recently when his illness and near-death episodes became too much for her to handle. She was working hard at just learning to be a teen. In her frustration, she said and did some things I know she regretted upon his death. Thank God, a few days before his death, they were able to share an awesome day going to the grocery store together. It was a sweet time between a daddy and daughter being silly—almost like normal. She was attending a rough inner-city school at the time and one of her main concerns was who would protect her with her daddy gone. I bought her a can of mace to ease her mind. A few nights after his death, God was faithful to send her a special message of love from her dad that reassured her none of the things she had said could ever stand between them.

Our seven year-old son, Ryan, had spent more than half of his young life at his daddy's side in hospital settings. He had seen suffering most kids his age can't even imagine. He had learned to be really quiet, just so he could stay with his dad. Some of his best friends during that time were nurses and doctors, who were in his dad's room on a regular basis. His older brother and sister were old enough to have started their own lives with friends and activities, but Ryan almost always chose to go to the hospital so he could spend every moment possible with his biggest hero. He knew his dad wouldn't live much longer and he didn't want to miss anything. When his dad died, he lost his best friend.

Jake, our two-year old was born in the midst of his dad's traumatic illness. He was a surprise. In fact, my husband found a new reason to fight to live long enough for this little one to remember him. Jake thought nothing of all the IV's, cords, tubes and hospital stays. He never knew anything else. He didn't see his daddy as sick. All he knew was Steve was his dad and he loved him. Jake was a very hyper baby so it was difficult to keep him in the hospital room for long. He thought nothing of climbing all over his dad and pulling out all those tubes.

I knew I needed God to help my children and keep our family going. God was faithful to each of us.

"I will not leave you as orphans; I will come to you." John 14:18

Your Story- Helping Children Grieve

He called a little child and had him stand among them. And He said, 'I tell you the truth, unless you change and become like little children, you will never enter the kingdom of heaven. Therefore, whoever humbles himself like this child is the greatest in the kingdom of heaven.'" Matthew 18:2-4

(Write about the children who have been affected by your loved one's death and how you think it is impacting them.)

_____

_____

_____

_____

_____

_____

_____

_____

_____

_____

_____

_____

_____

_____

_____

_____

_____

_____

"And whoever welcomes a little child like this in My name welcomes Me." Matthew 18:5

Helpful Input- Helping Children Grieve

Children and teens act out their grief in a wide variety of ways. Little children do not have the language to voice what they are feeling or even understand it. Adults have many conflicting emotions as they travel through grief. Imagine what it must be like for children. How a young person reacts will depend on the relationship they had with their loved one and what they are going through at any particular time.

I tried to be very aware of my children's feelings, yet I noticed they didn't want to share very much with me at first. They saw me hurting and didn't want to add to my pain. I kept reassuring them I was going to be sad for a while but I would be alright. They needed to know we would all get through this together. I found a grief group specifically for children. The counselor planned great activities that were perfect tools for the kids to be able to express their love for their dad and what they would miss about him.

I fashioned some great starters for children to be able to use in the children's version of MY FOREVER MEMORIES OF YOU. It is a companion book to the book you are going through now. Kids of all ages can use this personal memory book to draw or write in to express their many emotions. Each child should have one of their own to express the unique relationship they had with their loved one. Their memory book will be something they will want to carry through life with them.

When a loved one dies, the reality of death and how suddenly it can occur, hits everyone hard—including children. Their security has been shaken. Kids of all ages need to know you will be there for them. My children even needed to know what would happen to them if I died. So I made plans for that. When telling them about the plans, I let them know that I really didn't think I would die soon, but if I did, there was a plan in place and those who would care for them had already agreed. It put their minds at ease.

Fear often pops up where it never did before when surviving loved ones leave (even for a short errand). Children need to be told when you leave, where you're going and when you're returning. It's best to try your best to stay within those perimeters, or at least call and let them know if you're running late. All ages are a bit more anxious at separations than they were before. It will pass if addressed, and not belittled as an unnecessary fear.

Your home may be filled with a lot of whirlwind emotions that come and go as everyone makes their way through this time. Tempers might be on edge; then a new sudden flow of tears; then giddy play. There could be extra clinginess, fears at night, stress over activities that once were pleasurable. Some kids may want to be away from home a lot to avoid reminders; others may not want to leave because they need the extra security of home right now. Understanding patience goes a long way as your whole family works through your loss. Each child and adult will go through it in their own way.

A great time to talk to children is at bedtime when there are no other distractions. If your child had a bad day, you can ask if they are missing their loved one. Hopefully, acknowledging the grief will help them begin to see that everyone's emotions are raw and tender. Feelings are easily hurt. A blow up can happen over some trivial matter. Bedtime needs to be a quiet one-on-one time where issues can be brought out and acknowledged. That wind-down time can be a precious bonding between you and your children as you share your concerns and emotions. It is also important to just keep talking about everyday things as well. Let them know that life goes on and you will be with them as it does. They need to know you will not leave them.

Bedtime is also a perfect time to pray before going to sleep. Nothing else can calm and reassure like bringing everything to the Lord. He can comfort and bring peace when no one else can. Nights can be one of the most difficult times if you leave kids to muddle through grief on their own. Grief can be lonely but the assurance that God is with them will help them rest more peacefully at night. It will help you, as well. A stuffed animal with a photo of their loved one tied to it might be comforting to cuddle with at night. Some kids find solace in sleeping on their loved one's pillow or with one of their loved one's favorite shirts. They won't need these forever, but it can definitely help during the most intense grieving.

Don't get so caught up in your own grieving that you forget the children and teens. They might look okay, but they need your help in dealing with all the emotions. When you ask God to help them grieve in a healthy manner, it also helps you. Your family will endure and come out stronger than ever when you grieve together.

"Leave your orphans: I will protect their lives. Your widows too can trust in me." Jeremiah 49:11

Practical Ideas- Helping Children Grieve

"But you, O God, do see trouble and grief; You consider it to take it in hand. The victim commits himself to You; You are the helper of the fatherless." Psalm 10:14

- Don't assume children are dealing with the loss Ok just because they look normal.
- Watch for outbursts of emotions, and gently let them know it may be part of their grief.
- Also look for signs of withdrawal and isolation. They may want to escape into electronics, their room, drugs and alcohol (in older children). Gently try to get them to talk.

- Let them see you grieve through journaling, crying, sharing memories so they know it's OK to do the same. You need to teach them to grieve in a healthy manner.

- Go through the children's version of MY FOREVER MEMORIES OF YOU with younger children. Let them chose how they want to fill their book out- with drawings, writing, photos. Older children and teens may want to fill out their book on their own. Ask them if they want to share it with you but don't force them to. Look at it with them and ask them questions about their Memory Book. The children's version of MY FOREVER MEMORIES OF YOU has a lot more helpful input on helping children grieve.

- Tie a ribbon with a little framed photo of your loved one around a cuddly stuffed animal they can snuggle with.

- Make a pillow out of their loved one's favorite shirt to comfort them.

- Ask the child if they want to help you go through their loved one's belongings when the time is right for both of you. Share memories and stories as you look at different items.

- Find out what item of their loved one they might want as a keepsake. Let them know that you have to see if someone else in the family might want it. If several people want the same thing, you can draw names.

- If you think there's a chance they feel guilty about something they might have said or done to their loved one, you could open communication for them by expressing something you wish you hadn't said or done. Let them know, that it is forgiven.

- Perhaps they are sad because their loved one won't be there for a special occasion (like their birthday, games, graduation, wedding). Give them something special to carry on that special day as a reminder they will always be cheering them on. Children will often grieve again on important milestones in their lives when their loved one is not there.

"All your sons will be taught by the Lord, and great will be your children's peace." Isaiah 54:13

Interactive Work page- Helping Children Grieve

Children need someone to listen as they tell of their special relationship. All ages need someone to reassure them they will be OK as they go through a myriad of emotions. As you help the children in your life grieve, you will find you will grow through that interaction as well. I'm praying for God to help you and the children in your life.

- What is your earliest experience with grief in your own life? The death of a pet, grandparent, sibling, parent...? Recall how you felt? How will that affect how you help the children in your life now as they go through grief?

  _____

  _____

- What activities would you like to incorporate into your children's bedtime routine during this time of grief?

  _____

  _____

- List some experiences the children liked to do with their loved one. Which ones could you do with them to honor their special times?

  _____

  _____

- Which of your loved one's possessions do you think your child would like to have to remember their loved one by? If it is a special piece of jewelry or something too valuable for a young child to have now, let them know they will inherit it at a certain age. (Make sure others in the family know that).

  _____

  _____

- Many other ideas, activities and suggestions are available in the children's version of MY FOREVER MEMORIES OF YOU. Get a copy for each child to fill out with their own memories and stories of their special relationship with their loved one.

  _____

  _____

"Now then, my sons, listen to me; blessed are those who keep my ways. Listen to my instruction and be wise; do not ignore it." Proverbs 8:32-33

Prayer Journal- Helping Children Grieve

"He said to them, 'Let the little children come to Me, and do not hinder them, for the kingdom of God belongs to such as these. I tell you the truth, anyone who will not receive the kingdom of God like a little child will never enter it.' And He took the children in His arms, put His hands on them and blessed them" Mark 10:14-16

My Prayer Journal- Helping Children Grieve

(reminder- These are excerpts taken from my personal prayer journal, written at different times—all dealing with my children)

Heavenly Father,

Not only is my heart broken from my grief over Steve's death, but for each of my children. Each time I see them broken-hearted, it's like getting stabbed all over again. I had no idea how Jake would handle his dad's death since he was only two years old. When we went to the funeral home the night before the service, I had my mom come in case she needed to take Jake out. I knew the other kids and I needed more time. When we went into the viewing room, Jake was too short to see into the casket. I was trying to watch each of the kids to see who needed me. (I had purposely taken some alone time to be with Steve's body before bringing the children in.) Jake went straight to a chair and drug it over to the casket to stand on. He was so determined. Standing on the chair, he leaned over to look at his daddy's body. Although I had tried to explain Steve's death, my strong little toddler grabbed his dad's clothes and tried to pull him out. He said, "That's not Santa Claus! I want my Daddy!" We were all crying so hard, we couldn't speak for a bit. Each of the kids had time that evening to place something in their dad's casket and say goodbye. Father, how am I going to hold my family together? I need Your help!...

Lord, my shy son Ryan seems even quieter than before. He has witnessed a lot of pain and suffering for a seven year-old. Yet, he also saw true courage and strength in his dad. I know You will use this whole experience in a huge way in his life. It seems he needs to stay extra close to me and our home. At times, he needs an extra push to go play at someone's house. I just have to reassure him what time I will pick him up. He loves to hear me tell stories about his dad. When I do, he will open up with a little of his own. Father, please heal his poor broken heart. His dad was his best buddy. I lift up his teacher and friends, as well. I know they don't know how to help him. I see the sorrow and fear of doing something wrong in their eyes. Help me provide a safe, comforting home where my children and I can recuperate. Thank You for our church, schools and childcare families who are so understanding and supportive.

Father, I'm least sure how to help my fifteen year-old daughter Chrissy. I need Your wisdom and strength to help her. She was already angry about his illness and couldn't handle hearing anything about it. She still doesn't want to talk about her dad's death either. I pray this grief group will help her. She just wants a normal teen life. Our normal life was filled with crisis after crisis. Not long before Steve died, she got really mad and yelled, "When I grow up, I don't want to have anything to do with sick people!" She stormed out the door while her dad was in a wheelchair unable to chase her. I started to run after her and reprimand her for being so rude. You stopped me, Lord, and told me, "Just wait and see." (Twenty something years later, she is an excellent Critical Care Nurse who deals daily with critical patients and their families in life and death situations! Father, I praise You for the way You work everything together for good in our lives.)

Father God, my oldest son Eric, is on the verge of manhood. How can I teach him to be a man? I've tried but I can't. You will have to do it, Lord. I am incredibly grateful for all the ways his dad will be with him all his life. He's had the most time with him--watching his dad handle life as a man. Eric will be graduating high school soon, and moving out (way to soon after losing Steve!) How sad that his dad will not be there to watch him –yet I believe he is somehow, cheering him on.

Lord, almost every time we go to the grocery store, little two year-old Jake breaks my heart. He runs up to strange men and says, "My daddy died! Will you be my daddy?" Not only are the men speechless, so am I. I usually just smile apologetically, grab Jake's hand and move on. Steve's death has not only completely changed my children's lives, but it's impacted all the children in our licensed home child care. Most of the kids considered Steve a father figure. Not only am I grieving, and helping our children through the death of their dad; I am trying to help our child care kids deal with it. Today I drove a van full of kids to the park. On the way, I started crying. The kids asked me what was wrong so I told them I missed Steve. Then they all started shouting in unison, "We miss Steve! We miss Steve!" Father, help us all! Especially, help the little boy who keeps turning Steve's photo around. When I asked why, he told me he saw Steve sitting at the table like he used to during nap drinking his coffee. He knew he was dead so he is scared. Each child needs special comfort and understanding. I can't give them what they need on my own. We all need You.

"Now may the Lord of peace Himself give you peace at all times and in every way. The Lord be with all of you." 2 Thessalonians 3:16

Your Prayer Journal- Helping Children Grieve

"Praise be to the God and Father of our Lord Jesus Christ, the Father of compassion and the God of all comfort who comforts us in all our troubles, so that we can comfort those in any trouble with the comfort we ourselves have received from God." 2 Corinthians 1:3-4

(Ask God to help you have the wisdom, patience and understanding you need to help any children who are grieving the loss of your loved one.)

_____

_____

_____

_____

_____

_____

_____

_____

_____

_____

_____

_____

_____

_____

_____

_____

_____

_____

_____

_____

_____

_____

_____

_____

_____

_____

_____

_____

_____

_____

_____

_____

_____

_____

_____

_____

_____

_____

_____

_____

_____

_____

_____

_____

_____

"Because of the Lord's great love we are not consumed, for His compassions never fail.
They are new every morning; great is your faithfulness." Lamentations 3:22-23

8

I Need to Forgive

"For if you forgive men when they sin against you, your Heavenly Father will also forgive you. But if you do not forgive men their sins, your Father will not forgive your sins." Matthew 6:14-15

Sharing Our Experiences:

Unresolved lingering grief is often due to a deep hurt that was never resolved. It can haunt the griever and leaves them bitter since it appears there is no way to take care of it. Forgiveness is not for the one who hurt us—but actually for our own benefit. Carrying bitterness and anger around is like a vicious cancer growing in our spirit. It consumes us, steals our joy, robs our peace and leaks out poison. Even if we are innocent and the hurt was horrific, we still need to forgive. Every real relationship requires forgiveness. Perhaps the deceased wasn't there for you when they should have been; maybe they abused, neglected or deserted you. Whatever they did wrong was between *them* and God. Whether you forgive or not is now between *you* and God. Even if it seems there is absolutely nothing that needs to be forgiven. It might be wise to read this chapter anyway. Perhaps some of the things people say to you upon your loved one's death needs forgiveness. Forgiveness is always needed. There are many hard things about grieving. Forgiving is one of them.

My Story- I Need to Forgive

At the time of Steve's death, I couldn't think of anything I needed to forgive him for. He had been expected to die any time for about 4 years. Every time we said goodnight, or I left to take the kids to school, we both realized he could die while I was gone. Steve also had several experiences where he died and was brought back. After living on the brink of death for so long, you realize that the last thing you say or do could be your last memory. It causes you to live deeply and not leave things unfinished. We both cherished each moment like it could be the last. I couldn't imagine needing to forgive him for anything. He had fought hard and long to stay with us. He suffered intensely yet didn't let that rob him of living to the fullest.

A few days before his death, I had a fleeting thought. The kids needed new shoes so badly yet we had absolutely no money to buy any. I thought how unfair it was that Steve's illness had taken so much from our family. That thought shocked me. As soon as I thought it, I was upset for feeling it. It was definitely not Steve's choice to be sick. I know he felt horrible that his illness had made it so hard on me and the kids. I later realized that even though I didn't directly blame Steve (because he was one of the most selfless people I had ever known) that I still needed to forgive him.

Another time, after his death when I was left to face some huge financial issues and critical problems with my children, I found myself tempted to get really angry at being left alone to face life without him. Anger comes in many forms during grief and needs to be dealt with quickly before the sin of bitterness sets in. I found myself angry that others got to have a longer life with their loved one than I did; or angry at things people said while I was grieving; and angry that some of our closest friends left us in our greatest time of need when Steve had such a long hard illness. They couldn't handle it.

Though we all have the need to forgive, I have worked with people who have had to forgive far worse than I have ever experienced. Some have had to ask God help them forgive a loved one's suicide; or the person who murdered their loved one; or a whole missing family whose remains were found five years later (but the case is still unsolved). Some have had to forgive the person who died for mentally, physically or sexually abusing them during their lifetime. Some need to forgive a parent for abandoning them when they were young. Death does not relieve us from the need to forgive no matter how simple or horrible the deed was. It doesn't even matter that we were completely innocent and the offender was evil. Forgiveness is not for the offender; it is for us. It frees us to fully receive God's forgiveness and love in our own lives.

> *"Bear with each other and forgive whatever grievances you may have against one another.*
> *Forgive as the Lord forgave you." Colossians 3:13*

Your Story- I Need to Forgive

"Do not judge, and you will not be judged. Do not condemn, and you will not be condemned. Forgive, and you will be forgiven." Luke 6:37

(This may be a hard chapter to go through, but go through it any way. It is impossible to forgive without God's help. Our human nature wants to hold on to the pain and blame. God knows that we will only be complete and free when we accept His forgiveness and practice forgiving others. Write what you are angry about—then be prepared to forgive. There will be more on the forgiving part.)

_____

_____

_____

_____

_____

_____

_____

_____

_____

_____

_____

_____

_____

_____

_____

_____

_____

_____

_____

_____

"Bless those who curse you. Pray for those who insult you." Luke 6:28

Helpful Input- I Need to Forgive

Forgiveness is a hard teaching, not only for when you're grieving, but in any aspect of life. It can be amplified when you are going through all the emotions that can accompany grief. We may fully have the right to be hurt and angry. In our complete innocence, we might have been somehow violated. It is true, we have the choice to hold on to our bitterness and anger. Our hearts may cry out for vengeance. God will listen to our cries. Then He will patiently remind us that we still need to forgive.

Dear friend, you may be really angry upon reading this. You may be calling out, "I have the right to be angry!" "It's my choice to not forgive." "I will never ever be able to forgive."

You might be ready to skip this chapter or close this book altogether at this moment, but you always have the need to forgive in front of you. There is no way to fully receive God's forgiveness unless we forgive. There is no way to be free from the prison of hatred, irritation, bitterness and anger without forgiving. The lack of forgiveness holds us back from the abundant life given to us through Jesus Christ. When we hold something against someone, it is like an invisible wall that blocks the complete forgiveness God gives us. It deeply affects our relationship with the Lord.

I know what not forgiving can do to a person. When I was preschool to first grade, a family friend sexually abused me. He was a grown man who purposely perpetrated vile acts against a little innocent girl. He was fully in the wrong and I was clearly innocent. I didn't even understand, yet I knew it was wrong. I tried to tell someone but probably didn't know how to say it. Little did I know that un-forgiveness could cause such evilness to grow in my innocent heart. I was well into my twenties before I realized what a toll not forgiving took upon my soul. I looked fine on the outside, but there was a poison flowing in my spirit. It was un-forgiveness. It had spread to include an ugly bitterness against not only the guilty man, but those who I thought should be protecting me. It caused pure hatred and a sick feeling to well up inside me at the very thought of these people. This dark vein that ran through me had a strong hold over me. I didn't fully realize how strong until I was able to begin to forgive. I learned when you belong to the Lord, we are called to forgive those who have hurt us.

Forgiveness is much more than simply saying, "I forgive." (Although the first few times, that is one of the hardest things to do.) It is really impossible to forgive on our own. We need to ask God to help us forgive. He is the Author and Perfector of forgiveness. His love is so far above ours that He sacrificed His own Son Jesus Christ to take our shame and blame of sin. Jesus is truly the only innocent person there has ever been. God sent Him specifically to take our sins so we could live blameless with Him forever and ever. When Jesus was dying on the cross for all our sins, He asked our Father in Heaven to forgive us, for we didn't realize what we were doing.

We cannot live free from the effects of the sin of un-forgiveness until we let go of it. We were made in God's image- with the ability to forgive, as we have been forgiven. It frees us up to live more fully with God. Not forgiving (no matter how deep the crime) stands between us and the Lord. It also affects all our other relationships.

Many people find themselves angry at God when they are grieving the death of their loved one. They drive themselves crazy asking "why?" "Why did God take my loved one?" "Why didn't I die instead?" "How could God let someone so good die?" "How can I trust a God who let something like this happen?" God did not plan for death, suffering and disaster. He designed us to walk and live peacefully with Him for all eternity. Yet He also gave us free choice. None of us has been able to live without sin. It is sin that causes death, grief, sorrow, illness, violence. God will listen to our "Why's?" and then draw us closer to Him through Jesus Christ. He will not always answer the why? So we have to let go of the blame, questioning and anger. When we let go of our un-forgiveness toward God, we will find the One who will never ever leave us—the one who will bathe us in eternal life with Him.

You stand at a crossroad when you face the death of a loved one. We begin to realize the shortness of life, the forever-ness of eternity, and our need for a relationship with God. There may not be a real need for forgiveness for anything your departed loved one did. You may have already forgiven for anything that stood between you. If so, you are blessed—or perhaps not being completely honest. Even the very best relationships require forgiveness. There is no way any of us can live without either purposely or unintentionally hurting those around us.

Forgiveness becomes so much easier the more we ask God to help us do it. Perhaps that's why I felt like I didn't need to forgive Steve much when he died. I had a lot of practice before, so it became easier to forgive more quickly. Every single one of us needs to forgive and be forgiven. I'm praying for you as you face this opportunity.

"If You, O Lord, kept a record of sins, O Lord, who could stand? But with You there is forgiveness therefore You are feared." Psalm 130:3

Practical Ideas- I Need to Forgive

"Then Peter came to Jesus and asked, 'Lord, how many times shall I forgive my brother when he sins against me? Up to seven times?' Jesus answered, 'I tell you, seven times, but seventy-seven times.'" Matthew 18:21-22

- Look back on your memories of your "Remember When" chapter. Do any of those memories spark anger, resentment, hurt? Perhaps they are things you need to forgive your loved one for?
- Ask God to search your heart and let you know what things you are holding on to that need to be forgiven.
- Be willing to give up your right to harbor anger and obey God in His call to forgive.
- Realize it often takes more than one time to forgive. New situations will cause you to recall old hurts and you will need to forgive all over again.
- You shouldn't necessarily tell the person you forgive them. That's between you and God. Sometimes telling them will escalate the issue to a whole new level- like "Oh yeah? You want to forgive me? Well, how about when you did this to me?"
- Pray for those who have caused you pain. As you forgive them, ask God to bless them with a closer life with Him. Jesus tells us to pray for our enemies. Sometimes those we love the most can seem like the most hurtful enemy.
- Remember that our battle is not against flesh and blood (a person). It is against the powers of spiritual darkness (Ephesians 6:12)
- Anger itself is not a sin. However, if we let it turn into bitterness or un-forgiveness, it can become a sin. While grieving, you may be easily angered by what people say or do. Pray about it quickly. Pray for the one who made you angry and forgive them so you can be free from sin.
- If your anger is against your loved one who has died, you can still forgive them. They do not need to personally hear you forgive them.
- If you are hurt or angry by what someone says or does as you grieve, pray for them and forgive them. They probably don't even realize they hurt you.
- Those closest to you may not grieve the same way you do. It may cause tension or hard feelings between you. When tempted to be angry, chose forgiveness and prayer instead.
- Write a letter to God to tell him about how angry, hurt, upset you are. He will listen to your heart and then help you forgive the one caused it. David often raved about his anger,

the unfairness, his hurts to the Lord in the book of Psalms. God helped him forgive the very ones he vented about. David was "a man after God's heart."

- Use God as your filter to run things through before you speak or react in anger. Be quick to listen, slow to speak and slow to anger (James 1:19)
- If you are mad at God, let Him know. He already knows but is waiting for you to express it. Let go of the anger against Him and you will discover He is truly what you need.
- Write a letter to the person you need to forgive…then read it out loud to yourself or a trusted friend… then shred it or burn it.
- If you need to, write seventy-seven letters to forgive, read out loud and shred.
- If the person continually wounds you, put some distance between you. It is easier to forgive from afar.

"Get rid of your bitterness, hot tempers, anger, loud quarreling, cursing and hatred. Be kind to each other, sympathetic, forgiving each other as God has forgiven you through Christ." Ephesians 4:31-32

Interactive Work page- I Need to Forgive

Forgiveness doesn't just happen. It is a choice. Be willing to relinquish your right to be angry; and instead choose to forgive as God has forgiven us. You will be greatly blessed with the peace of Jesus Christ and a freedom from the sin of un-forgiveness.

- As you review your relationship with your loved one, what comes to mind that needs forgiveness?

  _____

  _____

- Is there someone who played a part in your loved one's death that requires forgiveness? (a doctor, a drunk driver, the person who sold them drugs…)

  _____

  _____

- List those who need forgiveness who have said something hurtful since your loved one's death ("It's OK. You'll have another baby." "God needed them more than you." "I know how you feel." "You can marry again." "You should be over it by now."…)

  _____

  _____

- What about those who try to tell you how to grieve? Or think they know what activities you should be doing? Or how long you should take to grieve? Write down those names and choose to forgive.

  _____

  _____

- Have there been family arguments and misunderstandings over possessions, money, property or the care given to your loved one? Write down what needs to be forgiven in these circumstances:

  _____

  _____

"Make sure no one ever pays back one wrong with another wrong. Instead, always try to do what is good for each other and everyone else." 1 Thessalonians 5:15

Prayer Journal- I Need To Forgive

"Try to live peacefully with everyone, and try to live holy lives, because if you don't, you will not see the Lord. Make sure that everyone has kindness from God so that bitterness doesn't take root and grow to cause trouble that corrupts many of you." Hebrews 12:14-15

My Prayer Journal- I Need To Forgive

(Once again, these are excerpts from my prayer journal—pieced together over several occasions.)

Heavenly Father,

Help me with this anger! Someone started a fund which a lot of wonderful people gave money to. I know they all wanted to help a young widow with four children. It was a pretty good amount of money, but it made me so mad! I was shocked how mad I was. Where were those people when Steve needed them so badly? I don't want the money! I want Steve back! Even as I pray about this, I realize, these people were there the best they could be during Steve's illness. They couldn't have paid his medical bills. They couldn't save him. They couldn't bring him relief or peace. Only You could do those things. Father, I realize they want to help the kids and I. I forgive those who didn't know how to be there for us. I truly am grateful for the generosity and compassion of all those who gave. Help me grieve with grace, knowing You are with me. Give me wisdom to know how best to use the money they are giving us.

Lord, the momma bear in me came out growling today. My mom meant well. She was going to help with the kids, and started making choices for them that were not her choices to make. She probably assumed I was too upset or weak to care for my children. From my usually soft voice came a strong and powerful explosion. I let her know these were *my* children and it was *my* family and she will not take it over. Father, I know my mom likes to take the lead, but I needed to set that boundary loud and clear right away. Steve may be gone now, but I will do whatever it takes to keep my family together and care for my children. Father, I need to forgive my mom for wanting to take over, yet I'm so glad You gave me the strength to make it clear that I will care for my children. I am trusting You to help me. Lord, as time goes on, show me how I can let my mom help—without taking over. She is part of our family, too—just not the head! With Steve gone, I know You are the head of our family.

Father, today I need You again. My daughter is having such a hard time with her dad's death.

I thought she would—since she struggled with his illness so much. She's making poor choices and causing great pain. I know she doesn't mean to. She is fifteen and losing her dad at such a critical age has shaken everything in her. Father, it's easier to forgive her for the pain she causes because I understand where it's coming from. I know her heart. I know she won't always act this way. The real challenge for me is to forgive the people who give me every kind of advice you can image about my daughter. I've had some infer that she is a bad girl and that I am not a good mom. I absolutely know that both of those are not true. Father, help me forgive those who give well-meaning advice. They are not living our lives. Help me be patient with them as they try to tell me how I should raise my daughter. Help me choose wisely who I speak to about what's going on. Put someone in my life who loves her, believes in her and knows that the way she is acting is not who she really is. That's You, isn't it, Lord. You love her even more than me.

> *"Whoever forgives an offense seeks love, but whoever keeps bringing up the issue separates the closest of friends." Proverbs 17:9*

Your Prayer Journal- I Need To Forgive

"We love because He first loved us. If someone says, 'I love God,' and hates his brother, he is a liar; for the one who does not love his brother whom he has seen, cannot love God whom he has not seen. And this commandment we have from Him, that the one who loves God should love his brother also." 1 John 4:19-21

(Ask God to help you forgive your loved one for anything that was left unsettled; to forgive those who hurt you now, and to let go of any anger you hold against the Lord.)

_____

_____

_____

_____

_____

_____

_____

_____

_____

_____

_____

_____

_____

_____

_____

_____

_____

_____

"And what I have forgiven- if there is anything to forgive- I have forgiven in the sight of Christ for your sake, in order that Satan might not outwit us. For we are not unaware of his schemes." 2 Corinthians 2:10b-11

9

I Wish I Would Have...

"Restore us, O Lord God Almighty; make Your face shine upon us, that we may be saved." Psalm 80:19

Sharing Our Experiences:

ANOTHER MAJOR PART of coming to peace with the death of your loved one is being able to express regrets. That might include things we are truly sorry for (wishing we spent more time with them, treating them more kindly, letting them know we are sorry for hurting them). Other regrets may or may not be realistic but still need to be articulated (If we had done something differently would they still be alive? What if I had made them go to the doctor sooner? Why didn't I tell them I loved them? I never got to say goodbye. Our last words were not nice.) We need to confess our regrets, ask forgiveness for the things we might have done wrong. As we lay out our regrets before the Lord, He will forgive and show us how He can still work all things together for good.

My Story- I Wish I Would Have...

When you live as close to death for as long as Steve did, we learned to live without many regrets. We tried to savor every single day. There wasn't ever a question of our love for one another for we told each other constantly and showed one another in every way we could since we knew our time was limited.

I believe Steve had regrets. As a man, it was hard for him to see the kids and I struggle financially. He was unable to provide the security and physical help he knew we needed. One time, he sat in a chair by our car instructing my son and I how to change a power steering pump. I know he hated seeing us have to do what he considered his job. He saw me on constant overload trying to keep our household running, caring for each child and him, picking up meds, caring for the children in my licensed child care home, taking him to the hospital or treatments, paying bills, mowing the lawn…

One of my regrets was always wondering if having so many children in our home was the best thing for his health. Yet I could see no other way to be there for Steve, our children and provide income for our family while ministering to other families. Children carry germs (lots of them!) Steve had no immune system to fight off sickness of any kind so even a cold would send him to the hospital with another round of pneumonia. Would he have lived longer if we hadn't had child care in our home? Looking back, I wouldn't change anything. It allowed us to have those years together on a daily basis.

Another main regret I have is when we backed off going to church. Steve's illness had him in the hospital so much—and many times he was far too weak to go to church. I wanted our family time so I kept the kids home many weekends so we could all be together. Our time alone together was so precious. As time went by, I think I might have slighted my children having the deeper support system of a church during such a critical time. We did have a lot of support from many people in the last couple of years before Steve's death. Having a loving church family full of Christian brothers and sisters proved invaluable going through the illness—and then Steve's death. The kids and I both needed that.

Another regret I lived with for a long time is that I broke Steve's rib when I performed CPR on him at the time of his death. When I found him lying across our bed, he looked so peaceful in his death that I paused before starting CPR. I questioned whether I should attempt it or just let him go. He had been through so much. I knew he was already dead. We always knew this day would come. I had learned CPR for that moment, but I didn't want to disturb his peace. I decided I would do it because I might later regret it. As I was doing compressions, his rib broke. Though for years I told no one, I was always haunted by the sound of his breaking bone and the fact I had done it. Twenty years later when my youngest son was an Emergency Room tech, he informed me that ribs are often broken during compressions. The CPR didn't bring Steve back and his broken rib never mattered except to me. However, it relieved my regret when I found out it was a common occurence.

Of course, his absence causes many new regrets. He never got to see his children graduate, go to college, marry or have children. Yet, when I slip into that regret mode, I realize I never want to bring him back from where he is. He suffered too hard and too long...and is free! He is enjoying a far better life than I can imagine and we will all be reunited someday.

"Godly sorrow brings repentance that leads to salvation and leaves no regret, but worldly sorrow brings death." 2 Corinthians 7:10

Your Story- I Wish I Would Have...

"But now, Lord, what do I look for? My hope is in You. Save me from all my transgressions."
Psalm 39:7-8a

Write about whatever *regrets* you might have- what you wish you would or wouldn't have done, things you wish you would or wouldn't have said, ways you wish you would have shown more appreciation, what you need to apologize for...

_____

_____

_____

_____

_____

_____

_____

_____

_____

_____

_____

_____

_____

_____

_____

_____

_____

_____

_____

_____
_____
_____
_____
_____
_____
_____
_____
_____
_____
_____
_____
_____
_____
_____
_____
_____
_____
_____
_____
_____
_____
_____
_____
_____
_____
_____
_____

_"Yet I am poor and needy; may the Lord think of me. You are my help and my deliverer;
O my God, do not delay." Psalm 40:17_

Helpful Input- I Wish I Would Have…

Having unresolved regrets is another factor that can cause you to stay stuck in grief. It is critical to express things you are sorry for, or anything you wish you had or hadn't done. Steve and I didn't leave anything unresolved. We were blessed to have years of warning that his life was going to end young. We both knew it could happen at any time. That changes the way you live and interact. Steve struggled with something for months before he was able to tell me. He finally told me when he was gone, he wanted me to marry again. In fact, he said it again the night before he died. I didn't want to hear it. I didn't want to even think about it. How could I ever love anyone else? Yet, later I was incredibly grateful he had told me so I wouldn't feel so guilty when that time came.

Many people don't have the time to make sure a relationship is as much as it can be. People have come and gone through the Grieve With Hope group (which I hosted for 20 years) who had absolutely no warning. A forty-something year old man was instantly killed by a head on collision from a drunk driver. His widow came through my group. One of the hardest things for her to get past was they had a fight just before he left the house. It seemed so horrible to her that their last words were so ugly. She couldn't even tell anyone about it for a while. She carried it quietly and painfully inside her until it finally came out. She was able to say she was sorry and she wished they had been able to say I love you before he died. Through expressing her regrets, she was still able to let him know she was sorry and she loved him—even though he was not there.

When my thirty-year old brother-in-law committed suicide, we all had many regrets. He had come to visit us the day before. We didn't realize at the time he was saying goodbye. We wished we would have caught the "out-of-character affection" he showed. We regretted not noticing the subtle signs. Perhaps we could have talked to him. He was so shy and reserved. Perhaps we should have tried harder to pull him out of his shell. Through the tremendous wrestling with our regrets, we finally came to peace realizing he had suffered quietly for a long time and was free. We came to trust that he was not alone; that God was with him even in his weakest moments.

When a baby or child dies, there are deep regrets. Death is always a shock (even when it is long-expected). Yet it seems completely unnatural for a child to die. Parents must struggle through gut-wrenching questions like: Did I cause their death? Why them and not me? They had their whole life ahead of them; What if I had protected them more? Did I leave them in the wrong person's care? Am I being punished? Why would God allow this?

It can be scary to face these regrets and questions. Sometimes people want to run from them and act like they are not there. It can be tempting to use drugs, alcohol, foods, shopping, travel (anything to numb or distract from the pain). That will just make things worse in the end. All the regrets will still be there, but will loom larger than ever because they were not dealt with.

Chances are you may not get answers to all your questions of "Why?" or "What if...?" As you express them and bring them out into the open, they are no longer bottled up inside building steam, ready to explode at any moment. It is critical to voice those regrets and questions through writing, sharing with a trusted friend, and best of all—talking to the Lord about them.

After my brother-in-law's suicide, my mother-in-law wailed and cried out "Why?" for about 6 months. It was heart-breaking. Then one day she calmly told me, "There is not going to be an answer to my 'Why?'" She was much more at peace after that and able to go forward. No one could answer that question for her although there were people who tried. Not even God answered that question. Yet she still had to ask it. After going through the struggle, she could finally rest in the fact that God was with her even though she would never know why the tragedy happened.

> *"Three times I pleaded with the Lord to take it away from me. But He said to me, 'My grace is sufficient for you, for My power is made perfect in weakness.'" 2 Corinthians 12:8*

Practical Ideas- I Wish I Would Have...

"Come to Me, all you who are weary and burdened, and I will give you rest." Matthew 11:28

- Write a letter to your loved one. Let them know: what you wish you would have said; what you wish you would have done.
- Apologize for the things you said or did that were hurtful.
- Ask for forgiveness for not saying or doing something you should have.
- Express the questions you need to ask such as "Why?"
- Realize you most likely won't get the answers.
- Write or express your concerns to God (Did I have something to do with their death? Would it have made a difference if I had done something? Why them and not me?
- Be patient as you wrestle with these issues. But be willing to express them.
- Well-meaning people may try to give you answers that might make you mad.
- Find a good listening friend who will let you vent without judgement or advice.
- The best listener and friend is Jesus Christ
- Bring all your thoughts, cares, burdens, sins, questions and struggles to the Lord in prayer. He will take them all and give you peace concerning each one. (Perhaps not the answers but peace)
- No one is without regrets and sin
- You don't have to live with those regrets and sins forever.
- Confess them to the Lord. Repent from them and He will make you clean and holy
- You do not have to carry those sins and regrets with you. They are paid for through the blood of Jesus Christ.

"Have mercy on me, O God, according to Your unfailing love; according to Your great compassion blot out my transgressions. Wash away my iniquity and cleanse me from my sin...wash me and I will be whiter than snow" Psalm 51:1-2,7b

Interactive Work page- I Wish I Would Have...

Write a letter on this page to your loved one to express any apologies or things you wish you would have said or done...

_____

_____

_____

_____

_____

_____

_____

_____

_____

_____

_____

_____

_____

_____

_____

_____

_____

_____

_____

_____

_____

_____

_____

"Create in me a pure heart, O God, and renew a steadfast spirit within me." Psalm 51:10

Prayer Journal- I Wish I Would Have…

"He who conceals his sins does not prosper, but whoever confesses and renounces them finds mercy. Blessed is the man who always fears the Lord, but he who hardens his heart falls into trouble." Proverbs 28:13-14

My Prayer Journal- I Wish I Would Have…

Heavenly Father,

As soon as the thought came into my mind, I was shocked by it. It was just one little sentence. "It's not fair to the rest of the family for Steve's illness to take so much." It robbed us of time, energy, finances, and emotion. The thought came as I was trying to figure out how to buy the kids some much–needed shoes not too long before Steve's death. I immediately felt guilty for even thinking it. Steve had fought so hard and so long. He didn't ask to have this disease and felt horrible for the toll it took on our family. I felt so bad about that thought that I tried to hide it like it had never happened. But, Lord, You know all things. Nothing is hidden from You. So I finally decided to bring it before You. Father, You are helping me realize it's OK to be mad at the disease and what it robbed from our family.

Every time I get short-tempered from all the tremendous stress I am under, You are always faithful to forgive me as soon as I ask. You give me the peace and strength I need to keep going with a clean renewed heart. Only You can do that, Lord.

Father, I wish I would have had more time with Steve. My life was incredibly busy in the worse parts of his illness. I had to keep everything going, yet I also wanted to cherish every moment I could with Steve. We did learn to savor everything in the moment- little 5 minute conversations, sitting on the porch swing, watching the kids play, listening to music… It was a hard way to learn to slow down and experience the richness of each moment. I grew up in a hard-working family with every second filled with busy activity. Steve helped me learn how to relax and enjoy life but he had to work hard at it. He wrote a song to me one time with a line that said, "Sit down, take your shoes off; tell me what you've been doing." I wish I would have learned to enjoy the little moments much sooner.

Father, twenty years after Steve's death, I can honestly say that I have no regrets. Whatever things I regretted or was sorry for has been washed away in Your presence. I can truly look back on my life and say I am thankful for everything. You took all my mistakes, remorse, guilt and questions and created beauty from each one—but only because I brought them to You.

"And we know that in all things God works for the good of those who love Him, who have been called according to His purposes." Romans 8:28

Your Prayer Journal- I Wish I Would Have...

"Restore to me the joy of Your salvation and grant me a willing spirit to sustain me." Psalm 51:12

Express to God your questions and concerns. Ask for His forgiveness for anything you might have done wrong. Ask Him to search your heart and reveal what needs to be confessed, repented from, and then fully accept His complete forgiveness and fresh new spirit through Jesus Christ.

_____

_____

_____

_____

_____

_____

_____

_____

_____

_____

_____

_____

_____

_____

_____

_____

_____

_____
_____
_____
_____
_____
_____
_____
_____
_____
_____
_____
_____
_____
_____
_____
_____
_____
_____
_____
_____
_____
_____
_____

"For as high as the heavens are above the earth, so great is His love for those who fear Him; as far as the east is from the west, so far has He removed our transgressions from us." Psalm 103:11-12

I'll Always be Grateful

"How can we thank God enough for you in return for all the joy we have in the presence of our God because of you?" 1 Thessalonians 3:9

Sharing Our Experiences:

Reviewing you relationship involves realizing how your loved one has impacted your life. While grieving the loss of their physical presence, you can celebrate how they have helped make you who you are. As you think about the specific thing you're thankful for, some of you may find too many things to list on these pages. For others, this section might be a little more challenging. Perhaps you have to really search to find things you grateful for. It could be the hurts outweigh the good memories. Perhaps you lost a baby or someone you were just starting a relationship with. There's always something to be thankful for. Thankfulness brings joy.

My Story- I'll Always be Grateful…

I would not be who I am if it wasn't for Steve. He came into my life on my fifteenth birthday and began impacting my life from Day One. I was a quiet reserved fearful little girl who didn't have an adventurous bone in my body. I steered clear of long conversations and got nervous when someone looked at me too long. Though I somehow had a lot of people who knew me,

I felt very lonely. Then I went through his line at the grocery store where he checked me out. Come to think of it, I believe he rushed to that register so he could check me out! My life began changing for the good.

We were a good fit from the very start. Long phone calls developed into a deep bond quickly. Steve loved to talk and I loved to listen, although he had a way of drawing me out with more and more conversation. He was a gifted story teller which showed up later in his writing and music. Even his daily reports of what happened were always so interesting. He was a writer right from the start. Within the first month, he wrote a poem for me which was the first of hundreds of love poems and songs he wrote to me through our time together. It didn't take long for this lonely young teen to feel loved. Steve bathed me in love and affection. I always thought I didn't know how to love, but I believe God used Steve to show me how love deeply.

I was always careful, cautious and conservative. Steve was adventurous, daring and spontaneous. He was always pushing me out of my comfort zone or messing up my carefully made plans. Yet he did it with love. I never felt forced to do something I didn't end up choosing to do. He would often come home and announce, "Road Trip!" I would struggle against it with all kinds of reasons why that wasn't practical—like not enough money or time. It usually ended up with a great trip filled with spur-of-the-moment fun.

Steve approached being a dad with much more fun and passion than most. He came up with all kinds of ventures and treasure hunts for the kids. Holidays and birthdays were always over-the-top. He took them fishing, exploring and on hikes. His made-up-as-he-went stories sometimes lasted an hour or more with the kids as the main characters. They were better than most movies. I always considered myself the boring parent who kept the home running while he somehow made everything exciting. I'm definitely now more spontaneous because of Steve!

I had given my life to the Lord when I was eight years old and had attended church every single Sunday. Steve had not really grown up in church so I considered myself more spiritual than him. A year after we were dating, Steve was saved and baptized. Like everything else, he dove right into his relationship with the Lord. Before I knew it, he was writing beautiful poems, songs and books for the Lord. It seemed his relationship with the Lord grew in leaps and bounds each day. Steve's love for the Lord and faith in Him gave him an even greater love and strengthened him for the suffering he would endure. Steve's faith in God had an eternal impact on me.

We were so intertwined that we both greatly influenced one another, but I always felt like I received so much more from him. There are so many things about Steve to be thankful for. In his too-short life, he highly inspired me, our children and everyone he knew. His life continues to impact our grandchildren who never had a chance to meet him. As you read this book, you are even being affected by his life--all because the Lord blesses and enriches what we do.

> *"I tell you the truth, unless a kernel of wheat falls to the ground and dies, it remains only a single seed. But if it dies, it produces many seeds." John 12 24*

Your Story- I'll Always be Grateful...

"Then I heard a voice from heaven say, 'Write: Blessed are the dead who die in the Lord from now on.' 'Yes,' says the Spirit, 'they will rest from their labor, for their deeds will follow them.'" Revelation 14:13

List all the specific ways your loved one impacted your life.

_____

_____

_____

_____

_____

_____

_____

_____

_____

_____

_____

_____

_____

_____

_____

_____

_____

_____

_____
_____
_____
_____
_____
_____
_____
_____
_____
_____
_____
_____
_____
_____
_____
_____
_____
_____
_____
_____
_____
_____
_____
_____
_____
_____

"When the perishable has been clothed with the imperishable, and the mortal with immortality, then the saying that is written will come true: 'Death has been swallowed up in victory.'" 1 Corinthians 15:54

Helpful Input- I'll Always be Grateful

Another important step in being able to go forward after the death of your loved one is to understand just how much they affected your life. Whether they were in your life for just a few days such as with a baby or a lifetime of marriage, the one you are grieving has changed your life forever. It helps you to go on to realize exactly what ways your life has been impacted.

Most of the time, we get so accustomed to a loved one being in our life that we take their presence for granted. We just expect they will always be there. It's such a shock when they die, we can't imagine not having them with us. Our minds, hearts and spirits cannot comprehend all we will miss about that person all at once. Yet it is a good way to honor them and the Lord by actually listing characteristics and talents they had that we are grateful for. When we voice our gratitude, we become more aware of just what a gift we were given in that person. And all good gifts come from the Lord.

Another wonderful benefit of expressing what we are thankful for is we can begin to see the things we want to carry on. If your loved one had a quirky sense of humor, you might choose to carry a bit of laughter on in your lives. Perhaps they were an excellent cook, maybe you might want to pick several entree's you want to make as a remembrance to them. Maybe you were blessed to witness unbelievable courage in facing an illness. You will be surprised how much strength you will derive from that as you face different challenges throughout your life.

Even parents of the youngest babies that have died can find their lives were highly impacted by the too-short time they carried that baby. Their lives will never be the same.

Even in troubled relationships, there can always be something good to be thankful for. Perhaps a parent was never there physically or emotionally for you, but maybe they taught you to change the oil on a car or showed you the right way to do laundry.

You might never have had the chance to tell them how grateful you are for the ways they impacted your life. It's never too late to let them know how much you love them, appreciate them and admire them for the best things in their life. You may think it doesn't matter since they can't hear you. Maybe they can. Even if they can't, it matters to you. Working through your grief is actually for your benefit—so you can go forward in peace. Realizing what they mean to you helps make you a better person because you're carrying some of the best parts of them with you.

Thanking God for the gift of your loved one will deepen your relationship with Him.

> *"But as for me, it is good to be near God. I have made the Sovereign Lord my refuge; I will tell of all your deeds." Psalm 73:28*

Practical Ideas- I'll Always Be Grateful

"Praise the Lord. Give thanks to the Lord, for He is good; His love endures forever."
Psalm 106:1

- Write a list of the things you respected your loved one for.
- Think of personality traits of your loved one do you admire most.
- What moral values did they display in their life?
- Which hobbies of theirs do you feel led to carry on?
- What traditions did they carry on that you might want to adopt?
- What did you learn from them?
- What were a few of their good habits you appreciated?
- Consider what your life might have been like if you had never known your loved one.
- What sacrifices did they make for you?
- How did they bring joy to your life?
- What was so special about your relationship?
- What acts of love did they share with you?
- How were they different from you?
- What similarities did you share?
- What kind of impact have they made on your life?
- What do you hope to carry on?

"You turned my wailing into dancing; You removed my sackcloth and clothed me with joy,
that my heart may sing to You and not be silent. O Lord my God, I will give You thanks
forever." Psalm 30:11-12

Interactive Work page- I'll Always be Grateful

> *"This is love: not that we loved God, but that He loved us and sent His Son as an atoning sacrifice for our sins. Dear friends, since God so loved us, we also ought to love one another."*
> *1 John 4:10-11*

Using the questions in the Practical Help section, write a letter to your loved one to tell them all the ways you are grateful for their life. Let them know how they impacted your life and what you hope to take forward with you.

_____

_____

_____

_____

_____

_____

_____

_____

_____

_____

_____

_____

_____

_____

_____

_____

_____

_____

_____

_____

_____

_____

_____

_____

_____

_____

_____

_____

_____

_____

_____

_____

_____

_____

_____

_____

_____

_____

_____

_____

_____

_____

_____

_____

_____

"A good name is better than fine perfume, and the day of death better than the day of birth." Ecclesiastes 7:1

Prayer Journal- I'll Always be Grateful

"I love the Lord, for He heard my voice: He heard my cry for mercy. Because He turned His ear to me, I will call on Him as long as I live. The chords of death entangled me, the anguish of the grave came upon me; I was overcome by trouble and sorrow. Then I called on the name of the Lord: 'O Lord, save me!' The Lord is gracious and righteous; our God is full of compassion. The Lord protects the simplehearted; when I was in great need, He saved me." Psalm 116:1-6

My Prayer Journal- I'll Always be Grateful

Heavenly Father,

You used Steve to show me Your great love. I never knew someone could care so deeply about me. You brought him to me at a very young age so I might savor all the benefits of his companionship. Everyone thought we were way too serious at a young age. I am so grateful we married early since Steve ended up dying young. Many people tried to talk us out of our commitment to one another. Once, not long before we were engaged, someone almost had me talked into breaking up with Steve. It was one of the saddest, most critical times in our relationship. I went so far as to tell him I felt like we should break up and see other people. It broke his heart so badly. I'd never seen him weep like that before. As he was crying, I heard Your voice say, "He's going to need you." From that time on, there was no doubt that I was to stay with him forever. Little did I know how much he would need me in the future.

We experienced many trials and joys together as a team. I recall his mom telling me after his death (after almost 18 years of marriage) she no longer thought of her son on his own. It was always "Steve and Eva." We built a business together and lost it; we had four wonderful children together which further enlarged our love; we shared ministry work together, we homesteaded some land together and lost it with our business, we had a fire in our home and rebuilt, were rocked by his brother's suicide, owed money far beyond our means, were blessed to see what You gave him to write every day through poem, songs and books, faced Steve's long term traumatic illness (with almost unbelievable suffering an no insurance), ran a licensed child care together in our home in the midst of his illness, endured several times when Steve was brought back from death and put on life support. Father, I am incredibly grateful for every single moment I had with Steve. I wouldn't want to trade any of it for it is all so beautiful. You were always in the middle of it.

Lord, I'm extremely grateful for the writing You gave Steve. I wanted so badly for his work to be published but too much of life happened. It's always been written in my heart. It's a huge part of who I am. He wrote a novel he called the Unknown Prophet about a man in biblical time who traveled the roads to share Your word with others. At the end of the first book, he meets another man who traveled with him until the prophet dies. He wrote a sequel about the second man who took up the word and continued in his work to spread Your word. I always felt like the Unknown Prophet was Steve, but always wondered who the second man was. Father, it wasn't until after I remarried that my second husband Dwight encouraged me to write. I never even thought about it when Steve was alive. Since that time I have written a lot. One day, it occurred to me that I was the second person, carrying Your word on to whoever will listen.

Father, thank You for Your word and Your love that lived so strongly in Steve and has been passed on to me and my children to carry on. Thank You that Your love can be carried by those who go through this book and that they can carry on the love they shared with their loved one. Father God, Your love is truly eternal!

> *"Let the peace of Christ rule in your hearts, since as members of one body you were called to peace. And be thankful. Let the word of Christ dwell in you richly as you teach and admonish one another with all wisdom, and as you sing psalms, hymns and spiritual songs with gratitude in your hearts to God. And whatever you do, whether in word or deed, do it all in the name of the Lord Jesus, giving thanks to God through Him." Colossians 3:15–17*

Your Prayer Journal- I'll Always be Grateful

"We always thank God for all of you, mentioning you in our prayers. We continually remember before our God and Father your work produced by faith, your labor prompted by love, and your endurance inspired by hope in our Lord Jesus Christ." 1 Thessalonians 1:2-3

Write a letter to God thanking Him for your loved one and all the ways He used them in your life…

_____

_____

_____

_____

_____

_____

_____

_____

_____

_____

_____

_____

_____

_____

_____

_____

_____

_____

_____

_____

_____
_____
_____
_____
_____
_____
_____
_____
_____
_____
_____
_____
_____
_____
_____
_____
_____
_____
_____
_____
_____
_____
_____
_____

"Through Jesus, therefore, let us continually offer to God a sacrifice of praise- the fruit of lips that confess His name." Hebrews 13:15

11

Where Are You Now?

"Do not let your hearts be troubled. Trust in God; trust also in Me. In My Father's house are many rooms; if it were not so, I would have told you. I am going there to prepare a place for you. And if I go and prepare a place for you, I will come back and take you to be with Me that you also may be where I am." John 14:1-3

Sharing Our Experiences:

WE MAY HAVE stood beside our loved one's bed as they took the last breath; or perhaps we got a shocking phone call that they were already gone. We might have held our baby in our arms as they passed from this life; or we could have received news they were killed on foreign ground. They were alive and breathing one moment, and then in an instant, they took one last breath and were gone… but where did they go? We can be totally absorbed with living our earthly life, but the death of a loved one causes us to look past this mortal life into things eternal. This chapter will not contain all the answers you might want, but will take peeks into an eternal life that is far more wonderful than we can imagine.

My Story- Where Are You Now?

A year before Steve's death, on New Year's Eve, Steve "died" in my arms as a hospital code team had been called in to save him. The hospital room was filled with his doctor and many uniformed people all positioned to work on him. Steve had been unresponsive for over 24 hours when his vitals started plummeting. They asked me to remove a necklace from his neck so they could do an emergency Xray. I lifted his head in my arms to take off the medallion that read, "May the Lord watch between me and thee while we are absent one from the other." I wore the matching part. As I lifted Steve's head, he opened his eyes and looked up past the ceiling into heaven, then "died" in my arms. It seemed time stood still… Everyone looked at me. I broke into hysterical sobs. Then someone grabbed my waist to escort me to a nearby tiny family room and left me by myself. As I calmed from my hysteria, I started making calls to my mom and Steve's mom, letting them know he had died. In the middle of a phone conversation, I saw a team on all sides of a stretcher whiz by the door down the hall. I soon found out they were rushing Steve to ICU to put him on life support. He was alive!

After Steve had been on life support for a while, he couldn't talk due to the respirator. He scribbled on the clipboard they had given him that when he was able to talk, he wanted to tell me something that happened the day he "died." Over a month later, he told me he had gone to heaven that day. I wanted to know every detail. My 36 year old writer/husband who had always used words to beautifully describe anything, could only keep saying, "I never knew God gave so much when He gave His Son." Steve tried to explain the beauty, freedom and peace he experienced yet words were inadequate. He was never afraid of dying from that point on. He knew where he was going and who he would be with. I could only experience the reality and beauty of where he was going through my faith in the Lord and belief in my husband's testimony. Life does not end with the death of our body. It opens up a whole new beginning.

God's timing is amazing. Right as I was beginning to write this chapter, my 30 year old daughter called to tell me she just found out she was working with her long-lost friend from church, Chiffon, at her new job. They had been friends when they were twelve years old, right when Chiffon's mother Toni was placed on hospice care. I stepped in to care for Toni who had become paralyzed from the waist down from the brain tumors which had metastasized from her breast cancer. I cared for her during the day and rounded up teams of volunteers to take turns during the evening and weekends. Her parents stayed with her overnight, also caring for Chiffon. As you can imagine, Toni and I became very close as we faced her last 6 months together.

One day, she was filled with fear about her approaching death. I tried to calm her by telling her how Steve had found God's peace as he faced death, but nothing I said calmed her. Finally, I prayed with her, asking God to give her the kind of peace I could not. She finally fell asleep in her hospital bed which was in her living room. I sat beside her, reading and holding her hand. She suddenly woke up and looked straight up through the skylight above her bed. She was obviously looking past it into heaven. Her face was glowing with tears of pure joy running down her face. Without ever taking her eyes off what she was seeing, she told me, "Eva, look how beautiful it is!" I told her I couldn't see it. She wanted so badly for me to experience what she was seeing. She told me, "Just crawl up onto the bed, and you can see it!" Toni couldn't take her gaze away from the majesty of what she saw. Again through tears on my face, I told her I couldn't see it. Then she said, "Just crawl into my body and see through my eyes!" I told her I didn't think I was supposed to see it yet. It was enough to see the glory on her face to know how real heaven was. She was never afraid of dying after that. I know where she is and who she is with.

"But Stephen, full of the Holy Spirit, looked up to heaven and saw the glory of God, and Jesus standing at the right hand of God. 'Look,' he said. 'I see heaven open and the Son of Man standing at the right hand of God.'" Acts 7:55-56 (Stephen's view just before he was stoned to death)

Your Story- Where Are You Now?

"He has made everything beautiful in its time. He has also set eternity in the hearts of men; yet they cannot fathom what God has done from beginning to end." Ecclesiastes 3:11

You may or may not have had a peek at heaven through the eyes of your loved one. Write about your thoughts about life after death. You know firsthand what it is like to have your loved one there one minute and gone the next. Do you know where they are and who they are with? Even if you don't know for sure about your loved one, do you know where you will be upon your death and who you will be with?

_____

_____

_____

_____

_____

_____

_____

_____

_____

_____

_____

_____

_____

_____

_____

_____

_____

_____

_____

_____

_____

_____

_____

_____

_____

_____

_____

_____

_____

_____

_____

_____

_____

_____

_____

_____

_____

_____

_____

_____

_____

_____

_____

_____

_____

"How lovely is Your dwelling place, O Lord Almighty! My soul yearns, even faints, for the courts of the Lord; my heart and my flesh cry out for the Living God." Psalm 84:1-2

Helpful Input- Where Are You Now?

There is nothing like the death of a loved one that causes you to realize how very real death is…and how really short life can be. Death is harsh and shocking. Our minds know we will die someday. Yet it always seems far off or something that happens to someone else. We are never quite prepared for it. Even though we knew for several years that Steve would die young, it was still a shock when it actually happened. I suppose he had lived through so much, I thought he would somehow always make it through the next bout.

God did not design us to die. He created us to live forever with Him. We were made to walk in the garden with Him, to converse with Him, to share our lives with Him and to love Him forever without end. Our lives were to be filled with the joy of His presence; overflowing with the richness of His love. However, the Lord created us in His image, with freedom to choose. Right from the start, Adam and Eve chose their own will, what God had warned them against. They wanted what they shouldn't have. Sin entered our world from that point and has been passed down through our spiritual DNA through the ages. We would like to blame Adam and Eve, but we all choose sin. We all want our own way. We all choose what we shouldn't and separate ourselves from an unblemished relationship with God Almighty, the very One who created us and breathed life into us. God warned from the very start that sin caused death. Adam and Eve didn't believe Him and we still don't believe Him. That's why death is such a shock.

Yet God loves us so much that He designed a way back to eternal life with Him. The way back to eternal life requires a choice as well. There's no way we could ever acquire that eternal intimacy with God again on our own. There is no way we could wash away our sin and return to His holy presence. There is no way we could ever earn, buy, steal, or work our way into eternal life. There is only one way…and God planned it and provided it. He sent His very own Son Jesus Christ to humble Himself and be born as one of us; to live in this sinful world and yet, not ever sin; to be willing to die in our place as a punishment for our sin even though He was pure and holy; and to be resurrected so we, too, could live in new holy eternal life. In other words, God sacrificed His Son so we could live in His holy presence for all eternity. We must make a choice to believe in God's loving sacrifice made for us.

Perhaps you had a baby or young child die, and you question where they are because they were not capable of making a choice to believe in God's Son. Jesus makes it clear that the Kingdom of Heaven belongs to little children such as these (Matthew 19:14).

Maybe your loved one never spoke about the Lord, so you question where they are. No one knows what happens in the last moments of death. I have heard people recover from comas who experienced surrendering their life to the Lord. You may never know with certainty, but You can trust in God's tender mercy and grace. He desires even more than you that not even one should perish. God loves our loved one even more than we ever could. We may or may not receive the assurance we want; but we still have a choice to make for ourselves. Where will we spend eternity?

Whether or not we have seen a peek into heaven due to the death of our loved one is not so important. Whether or not we believe Jesus came to overthrow sin and death by dying on our behalf is the most important choice we will ever make. We may or may not know if our loved one made that choice…yet we still each individually have to believe and accept God's gift of Jesus as our Savior. We are each responsible for our own choice of whether to submit to and follow Him as our Lord. Jesus came to give us eternal life if we believe in Him. If you are not sure of where you will go upon your own death, choose life! Choose Jesus Christ.

"Because you have seen Me, you have believed; blessed are those who have not seen and yet believed." John 21:29

Practical Ideas- Where Are You Now?

"For God so loved the world that He gave His one and only Son, that whoever believes in Him shall not perish but have eternal life. For God did not send His Son into the world to condemn the world, but to save the world through Him. Whoever believes in Him is not condemned, but whoever does not believe stands condemned already because he has not believed in the name of God's one and only Son." John 3:16-18

- You may have many questions about life after death, specifically about your loved one's life after death. Scripture will be used to address most of these issues.
- **What if a baby or child dies before acknowledging Jesus as their Savior?** Jesus said in Matthew 11:25: "I praise You, Father, Lord of heaven and earth, because You have hidden these things from the wise and learned, and revealed them to little children."
- But Jesus called the children to Him and said, 'Let the little children come to Me, and do not hinder them, for the Kingdom of God belongs to such as these. I tell you the truth, anyone who will not receive the kingdom of God like a little child will never enter it.'" Luke 18:16-17
- **What if a loved one died from suicide or in the act of committing a sin?** Jesus tells us in Matthew 18:12-14: "What do you think? If a man owns a hundred sheep, and one of them

wanders away, will he not leave the ninety-nine on the hills and go to look for the one that wandered off? And if he finds it, I tell you the truth, he is happier about that one sheep than about the ninety-nine that did not wander off. In the same way your Father in heaven is not willing that any of these little ones should be lost."

- This is not scriptural but from experience. After Steve's brother killed himself, Steve had a vision of Jesus with His arm around David, helping him say goodbye to friends and family.

- Steve had another vision. One time after a disgruntled employee went back to the post office where he was fired, he shot quite a few people before being killed by officers. Steve had a vision of all those who had been killed with their arms around the shooter, loving and caring for him. Things are much different in heaven than here on earth.

- This chapter is titled "Where Are You Now?" because as you grieve, you can't help but wonder where your loved one is and what their life is like now. Yet this question also is posed to you. As Jesus asks in Matthew 16:15: "'But what about you?' he asked. 'Who do you say I am?'"

Revelation 22:3 describes heaven: "No longer will there be any curse. The throne of God and of the Lamb will be in the city, and His servants will serve Him. They will see His face, and His name will be on their foreheads. There will be no more night. They will not need the light of a lamp or the light of the sun, for the Lord God will give them light. And they will reign forever and ever."

Interactive Work page- Where Are You Now?

"Now the dwelling of God is with men, and He will live with them. They will be His people, and God Himself will be with them and be their God. He will wipe every tear from their eyes. There will be no more death or mourning or crying or pain, for the old order of things has passed away. He who was seated on the throne said, 'I am making all things new!'" Revelation 21:3b-5a

What kind of body do we have in heaven?

"There are also heavenly bodies and there are earthly bodies; but the splendor of the heavenly bodies is one kind, and the splendor of the earthly bodies is another. The sun has one kind of splendor, the moon another and the stars another; and star differs from star in splendor. So will it be with the resurrection of the dead. The body that is sown is perishable, it is raised imperishable; it is sown in dishonor, it is raised in glory; it is sown in weakness, it is raised in power; it is sown a natural body, it is raised a spiritual body." 1 Corinthians 15:40-44

(Which perishable, dishonorable, weak, natural things in your loved one's body are no longer there as they now have a spiritual body?)

_____

_____

- **Can we explain what Heaven is like?** *"However it is written: 'No eye has seen, nor ear has heard, nor mind has conceived what God has prepared for those who love Him.'" 1 Corinthians 2:9*

List some of the best things on earth you've seen, heard or thought of? Heaven is far better!

_____

_____

- **Will we recognize others in heaven?** Jesus followers recognized Him after His resurrection. In Luke 9:28-33 Jesus took Peter, John and James up to a mountain to pray. Moses and Elijah appeared in glorious splendor. Jesus and the disciples recognized them.

Who do you hope to see in heaven?

_____

_____

"I tell you the truth, today you will be with Me in paradise." Jesus' promise to thief in Luke 23:43

Prayer Journal

"I tell you the truth, whoever hears My word and believes Him who sent Me has eternal life and will not be condemned; he has crossed over from death to life." John 5:24

My Prayer Journal- Where Are You Now?

Heavenly Father, today I was sitting by myself next to the freshly dug ground where Steve was buried. With my head hanging in sorrow and my eyes transfixed on the dirt grave, my heart became overwrought with darkness and despair. All I could think of was my own devastating loss and the anguish of my children. Over and over, my mind relived the horrible suffering Steve had gone through. Thinking of his poor body now buried beneath that cold dark earth was more gloom than I could bear. I feared I might actually drown in my grief. As I sat hopelessly sobbing, my chin was gently lifted by an unseen hand so that my gaze was now towards heaven. Everything changed! The sky was bright blue and full of hope. That peace that goes beyond understanding washed over me. My mind was no longer held captive by pain and darkness. As I looked towards heaven, I couldn't help but praise You that my husband was completely free from all the pain I had witnessed. I remembered our real home is in heaven …and Steve was there! What a wonderful thing to know for sure I will be spending all eternity with Steve. And we will spend forever worshipping and serving You!

******

Father, last night I had a dream about Steve. It began with him looking like a crippled 85 year old man, walking with a cane all bent over. Though Steve was only 37 when he died, I still recognized him and his poor body which had suffered several lives worth of pain. He disappeared and then I saw him again. This time he was young and strong and in perfect health. I was so glad to see him, I ran to hug him. I just wanted to kiss him and feel the warmth of his arms around me. He gently stopped me and let me know that wasn't important anymore…not compared to the riches of heaven. He asked if I would like to see heaven. I followed him onto a boat that floated down a spectacular river but I cannot recall any of what I saw except it was beautiful. I am homesick for heaven now!

******

Father, sometimes I think I will probably live to be 99 years old and Steve went to heaven at 37 years old. I know I will see him again but that seems a lifetime away. Yet when I compare however many years I live without him, it will be like the twinkling of an eye when compared to eternity. We will have much to catch up on—and we will have forever to do it.

> "Though outwardly we are wasting away, yet inwardly we are being renewed day by day. For our light and momentary troubles are achieving for us an eternal glory that far outweighs them all. So we fix our eyes not on what is seen, but what is unseen. For what is seen is temporary, but what is unseen is eternal." 2 Corinthians 4:16-18

Your Prayer Journal- Where Are You Now?

> "We implore you on Christ's behalf: Be reconciled to God. God made Him who had no sin to be sin for us, so that in Him we might become the righteousness of God." 2 Corinthians 5:20b-21

Write to God about your desire to have Jesus Christ give you a new holy life—eternal life. If you've already done that, ask to have more of Him to fill the void left in your life. Ask Him any questions you might have concerning heaven. Knock, and ask Him to open the door to eternal life. Seek Him and you will find Him.

_____

_____

_____

_____

_____

_____

_____

_____

_____

_____

_____

_____

_____

_____

_____

_____

_____

_____

_____

_____

_____

_____

_____

_____

_____

_____

_____

_____

_____

_____

_____

_____

_____

_____

_____

"Then I heard a voice from heaven say, 'Write: Blessed are the dead who die in the Lord from now on.' 'Yes,' says the Spirit, 'they will rest from their labor, for their deeds will follow them.'" Revelation 14:13

Finishing the Race

"Therefore, since we are surrounded by such a great cloud of witnesses, let us throw off everything that hinders and the sin that so easily entangles, and let us run with perseverance the race marked out for us. Let us fix our eyes on Jesus, the author and perfecter of our faith, who for the joy set before Him endured the cross, scorning its shame and sat down at the right hand of the throne of God. Consider Him who endured such opposition from sinful men, so that you will not grow weary and lose heart."
Hebrews 12:1-3

Sharing our Experiences:

"Again Jesus said, 'Peace be with you! As the Father has sent Me, I am sending you.' And with that He breathed on them and said, 'Receive the Holy Spirit.'" John 20:21-22

My Story- Finishing the Race

ABOUT 6 MONTHS after Steve's death, I was driving by myself to my grief support meeting. It was my first time to be alone during the evening without my children in a while. I was overwhelmed with sadness. I started weeping uncontrollably. I probably shouldn't have been driving. My very soul missed Steve so badly. I just wanted one more hug. As I turned the corner to access the highway, to my left was the most glorious sunset I'd ever seen. It stretched out across the entire sky. The colors were so vivid and tangible that I felt them actually encircle around me in a warm hug. It was the most glorious hug I had ever experienced. I carefully got off the highway at the very next exit which happened to be next to a lake. Finding a place to park, I sat there being hugged for at least an hour, watching the sunset change from glory to glory. I had never been enveloped in so much love before. As the sun slowly began to set for the evening, I heard a voice say, "I am with you always." It wasn't Steve's voice; it was the Lord's (But Steve was somehow there, too). From that time forward, I have always known the Lord is with me no matter what happens—no matter who else leaves.

Steve's work here on earth was finished. He had fought the good fight—better than most people I know. He finished his race and crossed the finish line. He was with me and now he was gone. I was left behind. I had spent some time questioning God. Why Steve was gone and I was still here? Steve seemed to have much more to share—more gifts and talents. Yet he had lived his life to the max for the Lord—now, somehow the baton had been handed off to me. I might have felt inadequate to go on without Steve, but I have discovered I am never alone. The Lord is with me.

He has been with me through my grief and brought me out into joy. He has helped me raise our children. He has given me wisdom and strength to face any obstacle that comes my way. He has given me rest when I'm too weary to go on. He even helped me pick up writing where Steve left off. He has helped me comfort others with the comfort I've been given (and now I pass it on to you). I will never be alone as I finish my race.

As I began going forward with the Lord, I became really lonely. Steve and I had shared all of life together. I missed being married, ministering with someone, enjoying our family together, sharing God's love with others, having late-evening talks, sitting on the porch swing… I told the Lord that I would be single the rest of my life if that's what was His plan for me. I told Him that He knew how much I loved being married. If He wanted me to be married again, He would need to pick the right man out. I tend to see the good in everyone and I might make a big mistake. I let Him know I wasn't going to look for anyone; that if He picked out someone He would need to put them right in front of me and make it clear that it was His choice. I did tell Him that it needed to be someone who would love the Lord as much as I did. Then I went on about my life.

Several months later, I was teaching an adult Sunday School class when a man I vaguely knew walked in late. He was going through a painful divorce. Immediately, I recognized deep grief. Part way through the class, this man told about God's grace in such a deep personal way that I thought this man knows the Lord. My spirit leapt inside me. I wondered what that meant. There was nothing immediately romantic—only deep compassion for his pain. Later, as our friendship grew, he asked me to celebrate his birthday with him. It wasn't until after I gave him my address to pick me up, I was getting in my van with my teen daughter, I told her, "I think I just got asked out on a date!"

After the first date, it scared me so bad to even think of having feelings for anyone else, that I told him I just wanted to be friends until after the holidays. (I knew the holidays would be hard). During that time, God reminded me of that leap in my spirit. I realized from that point on this was the man God had picked out to be my husband. Of course, there was much to work through. There were several times I told God I couldn't see how it would work out with so many children on both sides. God's answers do not change! Once He has spoken, it will happen.

Dwight and I have been married over 21 years now...actually longer than Steve and I were married. With God's help, we blended our families together. At the writing of this book, we have seven children who are married to wonderful spouses. We have enjoy 16 grandchildren and two great grandchildren. Life is an adventure with the Lord. Every day, we get to see where He leads and who He wants us to encounter. What a joy to go through life with our Lord God Almighty, knowing each day we can love someone with His love and every day draws us closer to heaven. We are running the race with the finish line always in mind!

> "Have I not commanded you? Be strong and courageous. Do not be terrified; do not be discouraged, for the Lord your God will be with you wherever you go." Joshua 1:9

Your Story- Finishing the Race

"Be strong and courageous. Do not be afraid or terrified because of them, for the Lord your God goes with you; He will never leave or forsake you." Deuteronomy 31:6

Write on these pages how you hope to go on. What will you take with you that you received through your loved one? Ask God to help you trust Him more.

_____

_____

_____

_____

_____

_____

_____

_____

_____

_____

_____

_____

_____

_____

_____

_____

_____

_____

_____

"Since then, you have been raised with Christ, set your hearts on things above, where Christ is seated at the right hand of God. Set your minds on things above, not on earthly things. For you have died, and your life is now hidden with Christ in God." Colossians 3:1-3

Helpful Input- Finishing the Race

It will happen slowly. One day you will find yourself making plans for the future. You might even be shocked to find yourself tasting joy one day. You might even feel like dancing! Joy is always so much deeper after experiencing the depth of mourning. Life becomes sweeter, more precious than ever.

You might realize you're not so weighed down by sadness. Things that used to seem monumental no longer seem significant. When you've experienced the pain of death, life becomes much more valuable. It affects everything.

The fact that life is short is now more real than ever before. You know just how short life is; how real death is; and how precious everyday life is. No one but the Father knows when your last moment here on earth will be. It can happen in a second, as you are now more fully aware. It can change the way you live for the better. You watch what you say to those around you, for no one knows if that's the last thing they will hear. From this moment on, you will have true compassion in your heart for those who are grieving. You will be able to comfort others with the comfort you have received from the Lord.

The air seems fresher. The sky looks more beautiful than ever. You don't take all the gifts you're surrounded with for granted. You are not in such a hurry. You don't fill your time with meaningless activity. You can begin to savor the simple things before you. Most of all you are free to savor the most precious gifts of all- relationships. You can love more deeply without fear and regrets. You can relish each moment, knowing God is with you. You can cherish all other relationships, knowing that everything else can pass away…but love remains for all eternity.

The rest of your life, there will be moments of grief when you will wish your loved one was there to share something. However, the thought of their new life gives you courage to go forward with your new life. Whatever you admired or appreciated about your loved one—choose to take that forward with you. Maybe it was their sense of humor, generosity, courage or strength. Make that a part of your life to carry forward. It can be your living memorial to them. God placed them in your life as a gift to you (however long/short you had them). Part of our gift to the Lord can be to take the very best of who they are to finish our race. Your loved one has become part of your heavenly cheering section urging us on to finish our race and join them with the Lord in our eternal home.

> *"When the perishable has been clothed with the imperishable, and the mortal with immortality, then the saying that is written will come true: 'Death has been swallowed up in victory.'"*

> *1 Corinthians 15:54*

Practical Ideas- Finishing the Race

"May God Himself, the God of peace, sanctify you through and through. May your whole spirit, soul and body be kept blameless at the coming of our Lord Jesus Christ. The one who calls you is faithful and He will do it." 1 Thessalonians 5:23-24

- If you don't have a church family, find one where you can worship, serve and become a part of.
- If you haven't ever asked forgiveness for living without God, do that now.
- Accept God's amazing gift of Jesus' sacrifice so you can live with Him now and forever.
- Ask Jesus to be Lord and King of your life. Be willing to follow Him where He leads.
- Develop a deeper relationship with the Lord through more consistent prayer time.
- Spend time every single day with the Lord. Believe you are never alone.
- Share everything in life with Him. Praise Him while you drive. Ask Him to find a parking place. Dine with Him. Go to sleep talking to Him. Wake up and ask Him to lead your day.
- Be honest with all your feelings you bring before Him. Let Him know when you are sad, happy, mad, frustrated, lonely, jealous, afraid, overwhelmed, weary, unsure, sorry, grateful, joyful... He wants us to share our whole lives with Him.
- Ask Him to search your heart and let you know what needs to be taken out.
- Seek more of Him so your emptiness may be filled to overflowing.
- Trust Him to lead you forth into the unknown.
- Be still and know that He is with you wherever you go.
- Ask Him to pull you back when you wander from His path.
- Realize that the Lord God knew you before anyone else ever did. He formed you in your mother's womb. He is with you now...and will be with you forever and ever.
- If God is with you, then who can be against you?
- Make certain you are on the road to finish your race. Jesus Christ is the way. God provided a way when there was no other possible way. Acknowledge, believe and put your trust in Jesus as Your Savior- the one who was given to give you eternal life.

"I eagerly expect and hope that I will in no way be ashamed, but will have sufficient courage so that now as always Christ will be exalted in my body, whether by life or by death. For to me, to live is Christ and to die is gain." Philippians 1:20-21

Interactive Work page- Finishing the Race

"...but I press on to take hold of that for which Christ Jesus took hold of me. Brothers, I do not consider myself yet to have taken hold of it. But one thing I do: Forgetting what is behind and straining toward what is ahead, I press on toward the goal to win the prize for which God has called me heavenward in Christ Jesus." Philippians 3:12b-14

*   What do you think God would like you to accomplish in the time you have left here on earth? (Hint: Matthew 22:35-40)

_____

_____

*   What do you hope people will say about you upon your passing from this life?

_____

_____

*   What do you hope to "hand off" (like a baton) to those still running behind you when you get to the end of your earthly life?

_____

_____

*   What sins, bad attitudes, hurts and regrets so you need to throw off- to lighten your load as you complete your race that is before you?

_____

_____

*   What do you have waiting for you at your finish line?

_____

_____

"If I am to go on living in the body, this will mean fruitful labor for me. Yet what shall I choose? I do not know! I am torn between the two: I desire to depart and be with Christ, which is better by far; but it is more necessary for you that I remain in the body. Convinced of this, I know that I will remain, and I will continue with all of you for your progress and joy in the faith..." Philippians 1:22-25

Prayer Journal- Finishing the Race

"'Where O death, is your victory? Where, O death, is your sting?' The sting of death is sin, and the power of sin is the law. But thanks be to God! He gives us the victory through our Lord Jesus Christ. Therefore, my dear brothers, stand firm. Let nothing move you. Always give yourselves fully to the work of the Lord, because you know that your labor in the Lord is not in vain." 1 Corinthians 15:55-58

My Prayer Journal- Finishing the Race

Heavenly Father, about a month after Dwight and I were married, we traveled with the kids to Texas to visit his dad. It was the first road trip with our new blended family. As soon as we pulled into the driveway, Dwight and his dad hurried off to spend some "man" time together since they don't get to see one another very often. I immediately started feeling sorry for myself. I thought, "Steve never would have just left me like that. Of course, I didn't say anything to Dwight about my hurt feelings. That night we slept in the guest room. I dreamed Steve came into the room and stood by our bed. I was so glad to see him again. He was just quietly present; then he looked at Dwight and told me, "He is a good man." Then he was gone.

I recalled the night before Steve died, he came and hugged me from behind and told me in my ear that I would marry a good man after he was gone. I did not want to hear it at that time! We stayed up late into the night talking. Steve told me he didn't think he could keep going much longer. It didn't seem like a new conversation. We had discussed his death many times before. But the next morning, he was gone.

On the drive back home from Texas the day after my dream of Steve, the kids were all busy laughing and talking in the back of the van. Dwight was driving when he turned to me, "I had a dream about Steve last night." I almost jumped out of my seat. Instead, I asked him to tell me about it. Dwight said we were asleep in the guest room when Steve came and stood quietly by the bed; like he was visiting. He told Dwight he was happy for us, and then left! Father, how I thank You for Steve in my life and for him blessing my new marriage.

Dwight and I have now been married longer than Steve and I were. Some of my children are now older than their dad was upon his death. Lord, You have used Steve's life, suffering and death to greatly affect us all. Far more lives than just mine and our children have been impacted by Steve's life. I recall Steve saying he was willing to go through the suffering because You told him it would help many. This book is just one of those ways You are using what Steve went through, Lord. Father,

I pray for every single person who ever reads and fills out this book to be drawn closer to You and eternal life.

Life is full of surprises when we follow You, Lord. We are not supposed to see all the twists, turns, valleys and mountains we must go through on the road ahead of us. We may not always have the same people running beside us…but Lord, You never leave us. You know the way. In fact, You are the way! Help me finish my life- the race laid out before me- in a way that honors You. Help me share Your eternal life with everyone along the way. I'm still running with the finish line in mind. I love You, Lord!

> *"For I am already being poured out like a drink offering and the time has come for my departure. I have fought the good fight, I have finished the race, I have kept the faith. Now there is in store for me the crown of righteousness, which the Lord, the righteous Judge, will award to me on that day- and not only to me, but also to all who have longed for His appearing."*
>
> *2 Timothy 4:6-8*

Your Prayer Journal- Finishing the Race

> *"However, I consider my life worth nothing to me, if only I may finish the race and complete the task the Lord Jesus has given me- the task of testifying to the gospel of God's grace." Acts 20:24*

Write on these pages how you hope to finish your race. Ask God to show you how He wants you to use whatever time you have left on this earth. What eternal investments will you make in the rest of your journey here on earth? Ask Jesus to forgive you, save you, live in you and go forward with you.

_____

_____

_____

_____

_____

_____

_____

_____

_____

_____

_____

_____

_____

_____

_____

_____

_____

_____

_____

"And surely I am with you always, to the very end of the age." Matthew 28:20

Together Forever
Written by Steven D. Hall

I have walked beyond the sunrise,
Its colors light my way.
I have touched the birds that fly
And touched the light of day.

The stars are my beacons.
The moon does warm my face.
Ahead of me there is a light
Filled with My Father's Grace.

As I touch the light of peace,
You are on my mind.
My love for you will never cease
For I leave my love behind.

I am still by your side
Thru your eyes you cannot see.
But I am there; I do not hide.
You will always be with me.

I will wait beyond the sun
Until we touch again.
Together we shall be as one.
With death, my life begins.

So when you cry, look to the East.
In the sunrise I do shine.
On God's love, we both shall feast
Together for all time.